HOKKAIDO I.

SADO I.
Aikawa
ware

YAMAGATA
•HIRASHIMIZU

ISHIKAWA
Kutani
ware
Ohi
ware

Soma
ware

FUKUSHIMA

HONSHU I.

TOCHIGI

•MASHIKO

Oribe
Seto
ware
ware Shino
ware

YOKOHAMA•
TOKYO

N

Treasury of

Satsuma

Sandra Andacht

Treasury of Satsuma
Sandra Andacht

First Edition, 1981
ISBN 0-87069-318-2
Library of Congress Catalog
Card Number 79-67717
10 9 8 7 6 5 4 3 2 1
Copyright © 1981, Sandra Andacht

Photographs: Daniel Stone Studios, Floral Park, New York
Drawings: Carl Andacht

Art Director: Marilyn Pardekooper
Editor: Liz Fletcher

Published by

Wallace-Homestead Book Company
1912 Grand Avenue
Des Moines, Iowa 50305

For giving me their love, support, and understanding, for showing great patience and for sharing my enthusiasm, I dedicate this volume to my husband Carl and our two sons Stuart and Jeffrey, our dear friends Dr. Elliot Evans and William Kimmel, and my late father Harry Simon.

Acknowledgments

The author expresses her appreciation to the following for allowing portions of their collections to be photographed for use in this volume: Robert and Gloria Mascarelli (Accent East Gallery, Bellmore, New York); Tom and Lynn Austern (Austern's Antiques, East Meadow, New York); the Kohut Collection; Jean Bernstein and Clifford E. Schaeffer (Flying Cranes Antiques, New York City); William Kimmel; A. Christian Revi; Charles and Evelyn Fendt; Ida Schwartz; and Steve and Rima Salwen. In addition, the author is most grateful to the following: Nancy Garthe; Cel Gelbard; Lincoln Mott; Leon Anders (Ancraft, New York City); Irene Stella (A Stella Show); Don Brown; Jim Leimkuhler; The *Antique Trader Weekly; Spinning Wheel* Magazine; Christie's and Christie's East, New York City.

Contents

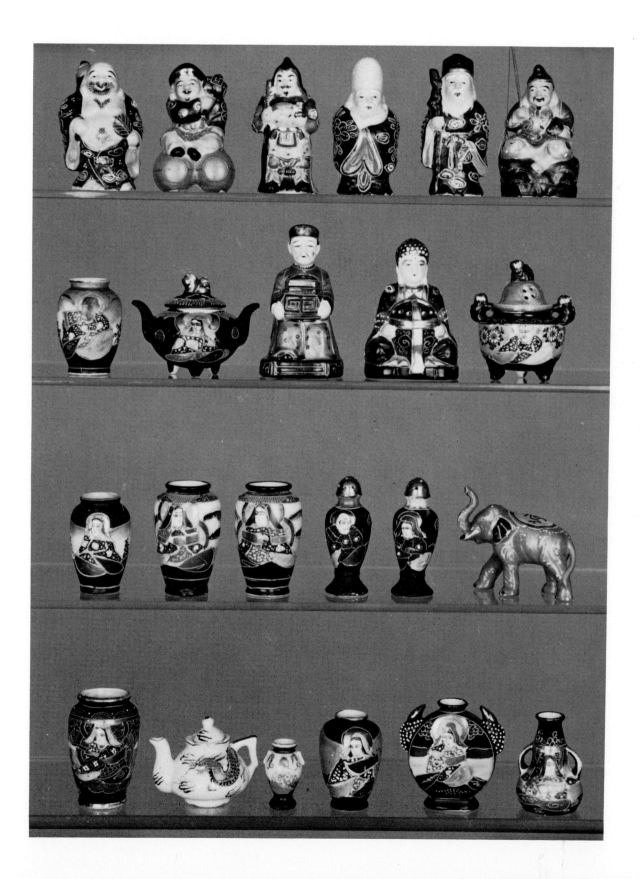

1 Historical Background

Japan is an East Asian country consisting of several groups of islands. The four main islands are Honshu, Shikoku, Hokkaido, and Kyushu. These four main islands are fringed by a thousand or so minor islands, reefs, and inlets. Together they are part of the eastern border of the Asian continent.

In the early centuries Japan was in contact with the kingdoms which we call Korea. In addition, Japanese culture was also influenced by elements of the Chinese civilization which included language, religion, arts, and crafts. Buddhism was introduced to Japan in 552 A.D., and with it began a new era of morality in both society and government.

The first permanent capital of Japan was at Nara, established in 710 A.D. It was here that literature, religion, and the arts began to flourish and develop. In 794 A.D., the capital was changed to Kyoto, and Kyoto remained the Imperial capital for over one thousand years. The aristocracy was cultivated and became sophisticated. It was a society where taste was pre-eminent. The government was under the rule of the Fujiwara, a noble house which intermarried with the Imperial family.

During this time, the government was concerned with privilege and ceremony, and there was neglect in the area of trade and communication. This system had manorial estates which were commended to religious houses or to a court grandee and, thus, were exempt from taxation. During the Heian society's existence, a new class arose, one which was of warrior nobility, and such did have lineage with the aristocracy.

Until 1600, the samurai were vying for power among themselves. Japan was divided into warring states until that time. Finally, a great victory was achieved by the Tokugawa family. The Emperor invested the title of shogun to the Tokugawa ruler, and the samurai helped establish a government of cooperation. The capital was set up at Yedo (now called Tokyo). Trade was encouraged and Europeans were allowed to enter Japan as merchants and as missionaries. Many noble families converted to Christianity, especially in Kyushu.

The Europeans quarreled among themselves over their ambitions for Japan, and distrust of the Church reversed the Japanese attitude toward favoring trade. The Japanese were sure that the only way peace could be maintained was through isolation, without the disruption of foreign influence. The English discontinued trade in 1623. The Portuguese and the Spanish were expelled. Only the Dutch continued to conduct trade on a very small scale, with one station on a tiny island in Nagasaki harbor. The only countries in which Japan had any interest, with regard to commerce, where China and Korea.

During the early years of the Edo period, the Tokugawa banned travel abroad, forbade Christianity, and virtually eliminated all contact with the West. The Tokugawa period (also known as the Edo period) was the period of the minor arts, during which perfection was strived for. The daimyo of the various provinces fostered the arts. Often a local daimyo established a kiln on his private estate, and the articles of pottery and porcelain were for his sole use and purpose.

With the shipping lanes surrounding the Japanese coastline, it was only a matter of time before relations with the West would have to be contended with. The United States attempted to establish trade with Japan in 1837. However, the American ships were fired upon and turned away. In 1846, Commodore Biddle made an attempt to establish trade, but he too was turned away. A third attempt was made in 1853, and it was successful. July 8, 1853, four American ships anchored at Uraga. The expedition was headed by Commodore Mathew Perry. Commodore Perry's "black ships," the *Susquehanna, Mississippi, Saratoga,* and the *Plymouth,* surprised the Japanese, catching them unprepared. On July 14, 1853, Commodore Perry presented a letter from President Filmore to Toda Ujihide, a local governor, which was addressed to the Emperor. The letter stated that the United States wanted the Japanese to change their laws, thus allowing free trade between the two nations. Perry returned a year later for a response.

The treaty of Kanagawa was given to Commodore Perry in 1854, thus establishing the opening of two ports for the purpose of trade. In 1858, the Treaty of Shimoda provided for open relations with the United States. Similarly, the Netherlands, Great Britain, France, and Russia followed suit, establishing similar agreements. However, the foreigners, the Japanese foreign policy, and the Japanese government found disfavor "internally." For the next ten years, there was friction between the classes, and the Tokugawa government was severely criticized. There was unrest as prices rose and the land was defiled by foreigners. The Tokugawa grew weaker as time progressed. Satsuma was a province with a strong army (having imported weapons from the West), as were Choshu and Tosa provinces. In 1867, Tokugawa Yoshinobu resigned, and the forces of Satsuma and Choshu toppled the government.

January 3, 1868, it was announced that the Emperor Meiji had abolished the office of shogun, thus bringing an end to the Edo period. The new government unified the country. The Meiji period (enlightened government) was the period of restoration. The Emperor took up residence in Tokyo (formerly Yedo). By 1871 members of the new government went abroad, and, in turn, foreign advisors were employed by the Japanese. The Meiji period presented a freedom to the Japanese which was to result in great creative and cultural changes, including industrial development and an increase in exports. It was at that time that the West began clamoring for objects Japanese, and at that point (for a brief span and to a small degree), quality gave way to cheapness, as superficial and mechanical specimens were exported to the West. This also marked the time that the ceramic artists of Japan began exhibiting in the West in large numbers.

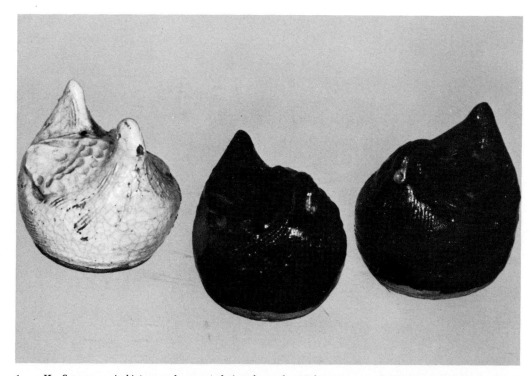

1   *Ko Satsuma suiteki (water droppers) dating from the 17th century–early Edo period. Height, 2¼"
(5.72 cm). Width, 2½" (6.4 cm). These rare specimens in the form of chickens were used on the scholar's
desk. They are containers for water, a few drops of which were used to wet the inkstone when rubbing the ink
stick in order to produce ink (sumi).*

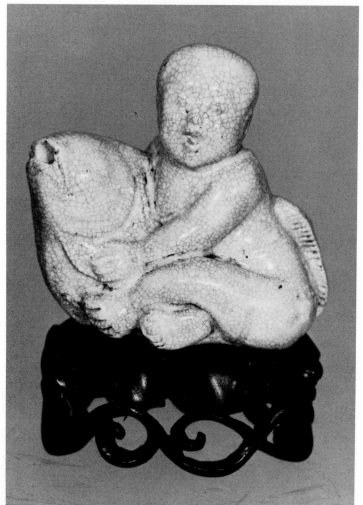

2   *Suiteki (water dropper) dating from the mid-18th
century–Edo period. Height, 2½" (6.35 cm). Width,
2¼" (5.72 cm). Another rare specimen, Shiro gusuri, in
the form of a boy upon a carp.*

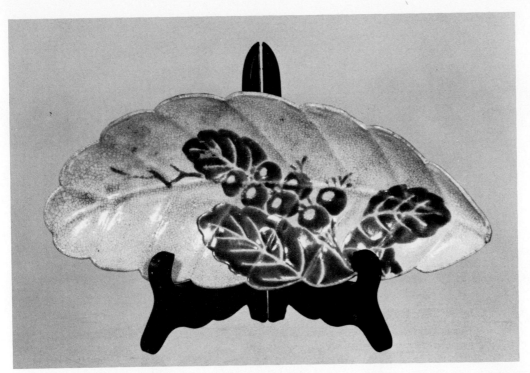

3   Dish dating from the mid-18th century–Edo period. Width, 9½" (24.13 cm). This dish is in the form of an artemisia leaf, Shiro gusuri, with monochrome gosu (blue) motifs of foliage and berries.

4   Ewer (saki pot) dating from the late 18th century–Edo period, c. 1777. Height, 5¼" (13.34 cm). Shiro gusuri, with monochrome gosu (blue) motif of Chinese style waves enhanced with an inlaid sterling silver (gin) quarter moon and highlighted with gilt trim on handle, spout, and rim.

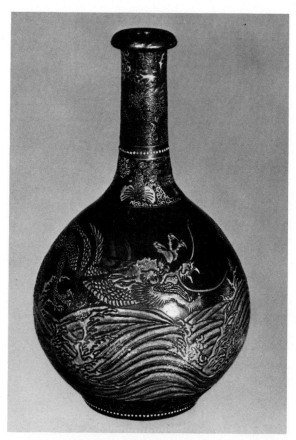

5   Bottle dating from the late 17th-early 18th century, but not decorated until c. 1830. Height, 15½″ (39.37 cm). The motif in colors and gilt is that of a dragon and waves, Chinese style.

6   Vase dating from the 18th century, but not decorated in its entirety until c. 1800-1830. Height, 11½″ (29.21 cm). The sprigged on ornamentation of branches is enhanced with green and white foliage, three plovers in flight (on the reverse), and gilt.

7   Bottle dating from the 18th century, but not decorated until c. 1830-1860. Height, 9½″ (24.13 cm). A blank with shiro gusuri, in a most desirable double gourd contour. This blank was reglazed and decorated long after it was first potted. The seasonal floral motif is continuous and highlighted throughout with sprinkled gold dust.

8   Cha wan (tea bowls) dating from the late Edo period, c. 1830-1850. (L to R) Cha wan, 4½" in diameter (11.43 cm), with an exterior motif consisting of six varying nishikide diapers forming spiral radiating compartments. Cha wan, 5½" in diameter (13.97 cm), with an overall floral motif which was carried over the rim and onto the interior. Cha wan, 4½" in diameter (11.43 cm), with bands of geometric nishikide diapers.

9   Saucedishes dating from the Edo period, c. 1800. Diameters, 4" (10.16 cm). Beautifully enameled in iron red, gosu (blue), black, and gilt.

10   Tile dating from the Edo period, c. 1830, 6" × 6" (15.24 cm. × 15.24 cm). Finely decorated with autumn flowers and foliage waving against a breeze and highlighted with gilt clouds of sprinkled gold dust.

13

11   *Tea set dating from the Edo period, c. 1850. The motif of cranes enameled in gosu (blue), paler blue, and iron red with gilt is striking against the creamy white crackled ground.*

12   *Vase dating from the Edo period, c. 1800. Height, 3½" (8.89 cm). This marvelous miniature is enameled with a continuous motif of cha no yu (tea ceremony) utensils executed in iron red, gosu (blue), black, white, and gilt. Its uniqueness is broadened by its contour.*

13   *Kogo (box) dating from the Edo period, c. 1790-1810. Diameter, 3¼" (8.25 cm). The motif of a sixteen-petaled chrysanthemum enameled in pale blue against a gosu (blue) and iron red ground is enriched with gilt.*

14   *Bowl dating from the Edo period, c. 1830. Diameter, 7" (17.78 cm). The interior is filled with fan-shaped reserves, each of which is ornamented with nishikide diapers and separated by silver (gin) inlay (kanagi). The exterior is decorated with a border of pink plum blossoms on a gosu (blue) ground. The underside has a central plum blossom.*

15   *Teapot dating from the Edo period, c. 1840. Height, 3¼" (8.25 cm). This traditional teapot (handle is at a right angle) has a sparsely decorated ground with a motif of seasonal flowers and foliage richly accented with gilt. The pear-shaped body is further enhanced with a nishikide diapered border on the rim of the teapot and the lid.*

16   *Koro (incense burner) dating from the Edo period, c. 1820-1840. Height, 9½" (24.13 cm). This koro is surmounted by a gilt Kara Shi Shi upon a tama, as represented by the midsection of this koro. The base is entwined with a dragon. The central motif of seasonal flowers, foliage, and flying phoenix is enameled in pale shades of iron red, gosu (blue), turquoise, and gilt. The base bears the mark Satsuma.*

17   *Bottles dating from the Edo period, c. 1830-1865, Awaji School. Height, 10½" (26.67 cm). Finely decorated in pale, transparent enamels against a straw yellow ground. The base, neck, and shoulders have gilt phoenixes in flight. The side panels are ornamented with turquoise and iron red dragons.*

18   Koro (incense burner) dating from the Edo period, c. 1800. Height, 10" (25.4 cm). This koro has a magnificient finial composed of open chrysanthemum heads, closed chrysanthemum buds, and foliage. The central motif on both front and back panels is that of a phoenix in flight against cloud formations. The panels are bordered with gosu (blue) and gilt five-petaled flowers on an iron red ground. This motif is continued on the outer side of the handles. The legs have half chrysanthemums (eight-petaled), foliage, and scrolls.

19   Vase dating from the Edo period, c. 1800. Height, 7" (17.78 cm). This hexagonal vase has an overall motif of wisteria bordered by a lower band of chrysanthemum head lappets and an upper band of paulownias and scrolls on a gosu (blue) ground. The motif is richly enameled in iron red, gosu (blue), turquoise green, black, and gilt.

19 A   This is the base of the vase in Fig. 19. It bears the authentic mon (cross and circle) in gosu (blue) of the Shimazu family. The name Issan, in gilt, is that of the artisan to whom the creation of this vase is attributed. The iron red seal is a potter's mark.

20   Mizusashi (water jar) dating from the Edo period, c. 1800. Height, 10" (25.4 cm). This mizusashi has a silver (gin) cover which is coated with a gilt wash. The pattern used on the cover is that of appliques of alternating kiku mon (chrysanthemoid form) and maru mitsu aoi (assaru form), with a chrysanthemoid knob having a center applique of maru mitsu aoi. The upper rim has a border of scrolling foliage enameled in iron red, turquoise, and gilt against a gosu (blue) ground. The motif of mums set against a defined crackled glaze is outlined in gilt and is highlighted with gilt jeweling in the form of clouds. The lower border of chrysanthemum head lappets encase gilt clouds and gosu (blue) fence work. The base bears the gosu (blue) mon of the Shimazu family. A further inscription explains that this specimen is a presentation piece. Pieces of this type were usually made for the exclusive use of the Shimazu family and were often given as gifts or presentation pieces.

2 Tea and Cha No Yu

Tea was brought to Japan via China at the beginning of the Heian period by Saicho, founder of the Tendai Buddhist sect. Tea was planted around Kyoto (the old capital) and became a popular beverage at the court of the Emperor Saga (809-823 A.D.). Shortly after 815 A.D., it was dispersed throughout the central provinces for cultivation. For awhile tea lost favor in Japan, as the Japanese turned away from things Chinese.

Tea was reintroduced by Eisai, a Zen priest, in 1191 A.D. Eisai was a founder of Zen Buddhism. The Mongol invasions of 1274 A.D. and 1281 A.D. brought a new awakening in Japan to things Chinese. By the 14th century, tea once again became popular, as proved by the tea competitions in which tasting and identification were conducted. Such social functions were attended by samurai leaders.

Cha no yu (literal translation — hot water for tea), known to Westerners as the tea ceremony, was developed by doboshu, men who were connoisseurs of the arts, during the 15th century. The emergence of Cha no yu in its simple form is credited to Murate Shuko (also pronounced Juko), 1423-1502, under the patronage of Shogun Yoshimasa. The wabi (poverty) ceremony was based upon Zen-inspired values.

Sen no Rikyu (1512-1591) was Shoko's successor. At that time, there were two forms of Cha no yu; wabi and that which was derived from the doboshu, a flamboyant ceremony. Sen no Rikyu, the foremost tea master, was responsible for the planning and execution of tea events. Under shogun Hideyoshi, Sen no Rikyu wrote a set of rules governing every aspect of Cha no yu, including the size of the room, the preparation of the tea, the selection of food, correct gestures, etc.

Japanese pottery and porcelain articles were originally produced for use in Cha no yu. The Japanese were particularly taken with pottery, admiring its form, style, and especially that which would be considered imperfections by Western standards: irregular forms — asymmetry and the impressions left by the potter's fingers or his tools. Such features were not hidden, but were accentuated. From the 15th century on, Cha no yu played an important role in the art of the potter. The tea masters were aesthetic arbiters, and they had a profound influence on ceramic production.

Until the latter part of the 19th century, Japanese ceramics received little attention in the West, as compared to that given Chinese ceramics. What interest there was at the time was confined to the various categories of Japanese porcelains. The difficulty confronting Western collectors and interested parties is that Japanese pottery production was, for the most part, a family undertaking, and the families moved about from one area to another, as did the master.

Among the most important articles used in Cha no yu are objects of pottery. The enameled pottery (faience) wares of the Edo period represented the courtly taste of the daimyo, and such included Satsuma wares as well as the Satsuma wares of the various schools.

The Tea Ceremony

The tea ceremony (Cha no yu) is a tradition which may be difficult for Westerners to understand. It is more than a refined pastime. It was the nucleous around which the various branches of art evolved, including the industrial arts. The manner (ceremony) by which the tea is served depends on the season of the year and the school to which the host belongs.

The host notifies those whom he wishes to be his guests. He will advise his principal guest (Shokyaku) of the names of those who are invited. The day before the ceremony, the guests will express their solicitations (zerei) to their host. On the day of the ceremony, the guests assemble in the waiting room (yoritzuki), where indoor footwear is donned and admirations are expressed for the preparations made by the host.

The guests enter the tea room, which is approximately ten feet square. This room contains a flooring of mats. The principal guest enters first. The host, already in the tea room, greets his guests. Once the guests are seated on the mats, the host produces kaiseki. This is a simple meal which is appealing both to the eye and the palate. Saki is then drunk. Afterwards, a water flavored with herbs and salt is passed around so that the guests can cleanse their lips and fingers.

Following a slight recess (nadachi), which allows the guests time to exchange pleasantries, a ceremonial gong is sounded. The guests return to the tea room and are served tea in a ritual manner. The host prepares the tea by placing powdered tea in the tea bowl (cha wan), adding hot water, and frothing the mixture with a bamboo whisk. In turn, each guest consumes the tea and returns the bowl to the host, who carefully wipes the bowl clean and prepares tea once again for the next guest.

The ceremony ends, and the host hands the utensils used to his guests so that they may be admired.

Among the ceramic utensils used in Cha no yu are
> *chaire* — tea caddy for thick tea
> *chaki* — tea caddy used for thin tea
> *cha wan* — tea bowl
> *choshi* — a saki container with a spout
> *koboshi* — waste water holder
> *kogo* — incense box or container
> *mizusashi* — water jar

as well as various *koro* (incense burners); *hanna ike* (flower vases); ladle rests; ash containers; cake bowls; plates; bottles for powdered tea; jars for leaf tea; brazier stands, etc.

21   *Koro (incense burner) dating from the Edo period, c. 1820-1840. Diameter, 5" (12.7 cm). A finely enameled miniature decorated in iron red, gosu (blue), and gilt with four panels depicting a dragon, Kara Shi Shi, clouds, and chrysanthemums between bands of diapers and half diapers. The lid has a central reserve enameled with a floral spray. Standing on four curled legs, the base bears the gosu (blue) mon of the Shimazu family.*

23   *Vase dating from the Edo period, c. 1830. Height, 3½" (8.89 cm). When presented in* Satsuma: An Illustrated Guide *it was thought to be a spill holder. Further examination reveals that this specimen was at one time a koro with a silver (gin) lid. Now minus the lid, this finely enameled item is converted into a miniature vase with a silver rim. Standing on three curled legs, each enameled with a ladybug, it possesses an overall motif of bands of nishikide diapers minutely detailed and enameled in iron red, gosu (blue), turquoise, black, and gilt.*

22   *Koro (incense burner) dating from the Edo period, c. 1830. Diameter, 4" (10.16 cm). This koro has a silver (gin) cagework lid. The overall continuous motif of maple leaves was executed in both monochrome and nishikide diapers. The underside is decorated with reserves filled with frolicking Kara Shi Shi. The base bears the gosu (blue) mon of the Shimazu family.*

24   *Koro (incense burner) dating from the Edo period, c. 1840. Height, 4" (10.16 cm). Similarly to Fig. 23, this specimen is minus its lid, which in all probability was faience. It still retains excellent value, even though it is not intact. This is due to the rarity of fine quality Edo period specimens. They are difficult to find and harder to obtain for one's personal collection due to their high values. The floral motif is enameled in iron red, gosu (blue), turquoise, white, black, and gilt. The foot is ornamented with minogame (winged tortoises).*

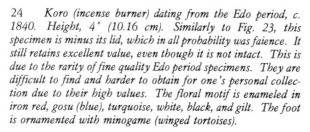

25 *Cha wan (tea bowl) dating from the Edo period, c. 1830-1855. Diameter, 4½" (11.43 cm). Height, 3 3/8" (11.37 cm). The body is finely enameled in colors and gilt, having an upper border band of nishikide diapers and a lower band of outlines of clouds.*

26 *Vase dating from the Edo period, c. 1840-1860. Height, 4" (10.16 cm). The motif of autumn flowers and foliage is accented with gilt cloud formations of sprinkled gold dust on a slightly fluted body.*

27 *Vase dating from the Edo period, c. 1850-1865. Height, 6 ¾" (17.15 cm). This piece has a rope tassel ornamentation around the rim, with a slight molding creating the effect of a drape or curtain. Not unlike other specimens of the late Edo period, the motif is that of flowers—in this instance chrysanthemums and foliage. Unlike most specimens illustrated which date from the late Edo period, the enamels on this piece are quite intense. The overall motif is highlighted with gilt cloud formations of sprinkled gold dust.*

21

28   *An important example of Kyoto School Satsuma of the late Edo period is the figure of Shoki (queller of the Oni) and Oni, who dangles from his loincloth. This specimen dates from about 1840 and stands 13" high (33.02 cm). (Pictured, Front Cover.)*

29   *(L to R): Figure of a seated dignitary dating from the Edo period, c. 1830-1865. Height, 11" (27.94 cm). Figure of a goat dating from the Edo period, c. 1830-1865. Height, 10" (25.4 cm). Figure of a crane dating from the Edo period, c. 1830-1865. Height, 13" (33.02 cm). All three specimens are painted in pale hues with gilt accents.*

30   *Figure of boy with fan dating from the Edo period, c. 1840. Length, 13" (33.02 cm). Similar to examples in Fig. 29, this objet d'art is three-dimensional. The rockwork and ground have protruding blossoms and foliage. The enamels are of pale hues with gilt accents. This object is very detailed and finely executed. The paste is close grained, and the crackles in the glaze are barely visible.*

31   *Tray dating from the Edo period, c. 1800-1830. Diameter, 7" (17.78 cm). The sparse motif is that of peony blossoms and hanna ike. The border is captured by two flying cranes molded in relief. The paste is hard grained and the crackle in the glaze is almost invisible. This tray stands on three legs and is finely enameled in pastel hues with gilt highlights in a very delicate manner. Although the motif is sparse, the overall effect is elegant.*

32   *Vases dating from the Edo period, c. 1820. Height, 8½" (21.59 cm). This pair of Kinkozan Awata School vases stand on double bases with a five-petaled flower cut into each lower base. Each of the panels depicts a varying array of seasonal flowers enameled in colors and gilt.*

34   Covered bowl dating from the Edo period, c. 1840. Height, 7" (17.78 cm). The pattern is executed in both pale and intense hues of crimson, green, turquoise, and gilt with blue used sparingly and only on the small blue birds in flight, which appear scattered in just a few areas. Finely contoured and enameled, the cover is topped with a gilt spire finial.

33   Vases dating from the Edo period, c. 1840. Height, 13" (33.02 cm). This pair of cylindrical vases are Kinkozan Awata School. The overall motif is that of peony blossoms, cherry blossoms, other flowers and foliage, and cranes in flight. The rim has a diaper executed in blue green and crimson with gilt throughout the pattern.

35   Plate dating from the Edo period, c. 1840. Diameter, 12" (30.48 cm). Marked Taizan, this plate is attributed to the sixth generation of the Taizan line of potters. The motif of morning glories and foliage swaying in the breeze is finely enameled in crimson, gosu (blue), turquoise green, and gilt with pink and gilt cloud formations. The cloud formations make the overall motif appear as if it were floating on air.

36   Figure dating from the Edo period, Kwansei era, c. 1790. Height, 11½" (29.21 cm). This superb figure of a seated "gibbon," in shiro gusuri has but the faintest dab of color (pale shading) on the facial features, thus enhancing it and adding to its lifelike expression. (See Back Cover.)

37   Vase dating from the Edo period, Kwansei era, 1795. Height, 7¼" (18.42 cm). The vase has a pleasing form with flared foot, bulbous body, trumpet mouth, and elephant head handles. This specimen is finely enameled in iron red, gosu (blue), and gilt. The motif consists of bands featuring diapers, lotus and scrolls, diapers with floral reserves, chrysanthemum lappets, and scrolls and lotus. The vase is further enriched by the expansive use of gosu (blue).

38   *Covered jar dating from the Edo-Meiji period, c. 1868. Height, 7"*
(17.78 cm). This handsome specimen has a sterling silver (gin) cover
which was covered with a gold wash (likely 24K). On the lid are alter-
nating appliques of chrysanthemums and foliage with a chrysanthemum
bud finial. The overall motif is finely executed in iron red, gosu (blue),
turquoise, and gilt. The body consists of four panels; the two largest con-
taining a garden filled with chrysanthemums and the two smaller contain-
ing flying phoenixes. The bordering band near the rim contains flying
dragons. Standing on four curled, bracket feet, this object bears the
signature of Genzan.

39   *Vase dating from the Edo period, c. 1850-1865. Height, 5" (12.7*
cm). This vase, although sparsely decorated, is most appealing. It has two
animal head ears and fan-shaped reserves (two on one side and three on the
reverse). The reserves are filled with flowers and foliage, birds and land-
scapes. The enamels are pale with gilt highlights and accents.

40   *Teapot dating from the Edo*
period, c. 1850. Height, 3" (7.62 cm).
This teapot, in Japanese tradition, has
its handle at a right angle. The motif
of maple leaves in scattered positions
throughout enhances the central motif
of a fan decorated with clouds, diapers,
and plum blossoms. It is finely
enameled in iron red-orange, green,
gosu (blue), and gilt. The base has
markings in gosu which read Satsuma
yaki.

3 Prominent Westerners

Ernest Francisco Fenollosa (1853-1908)

Ernest Fenollosa was an American Orientalist, educator, and poet. He graduated from Harvard in 1874. He pioneered the study of Oriental art and lived in Japan much of his life. He taught at Tokyo University, the Tokyo Academy of Fine Arts and the Imperial Normal School. He was the manager of the fine arts department of the Imperial Museum and helped establish the Imperial Commission of Fine Arts. During the time of his residence there, he recorded and cataloged the art collections of Japan. Due to his efforts, the National Treasures Law was enacted in Japan in 1884.

Edward Sylvester Morse (1838-1925)

Edward Morse was a professor of zoology at the Tokyo Imperial University from 1877 to 1880. His invaluable collection of Japanese pottery was purchased by the Museum of Fine Arts in Boston, Massachusetts, and Edward Morse was appointed its curator. In 1901, he issued the famous catalog of the collection. After 1880, he became the director of the Peabody Museum, Salem, Massachusetts. Among his written works are *Japanese Homes* — 1886; *Glimpses of China* — 1902; and *Japan, Day by Day* — 1917.

41   Pilgrim flasks (modified contour) dating from the Edo period, c. 1840. Height, 7½″ (19.05 cm). These flasks are attributed to Taizan, sixth generation, and are marked Taizan. They are not mirror images. Each has a central reserve on both sides decorated with varied forms of peony blossoms and chrysanthemums. The central reserves are captured by a border band of diapers. The body of each piece is entirely covered with "en gobe" (white slip forming fern and scroll motifs—warabide in low relief). The shoulders and side panels are enameled with mon and paulownia blossoms.

42   Vase dating from the Edo period, c. first half of the 19th century. Height, 12½″ (31.75 cm). The motif on both sides of the specimen were executed in "mezzo relievo." Depicted are scenic views of a mountain village, waterfalls, and flora and fauna, with a man and dog walking up the mountain on one side. The shoulders are enhanced with ringed, animal head ears. The overall motif of varied colored irises and diapers balance the ornamentation.

43   Bowl dating from the Edo period, c. 1830. Diameter, 6¼" (15.87 cm). An elegant motif finely enameled on the interior in iron red, gosu (blue), black, and gilt. The exterior has a small band of diapers near the foot trim.

44   Bowl dating from the Edo period, c. 1830. Diameter, 6¼" (15.87 cm). With a variation on the interior ornamentation, it is executed in the same hues and in the same manner as that in Fig. 43.

45   Vase dating from the Edo period, second quarter of the 19th century. Height, 5¾" (14.6 cm). Finely enameled in iron red, gosu (blue), turquoise green, and gilt with chrysanthemums and foliage between chrysanthemum head lappets. There is an applied lizard at the neck. The base bears the gosu (blue) mon of the Shimazu family.

47   Tray dating from the Edo period, third quarter of the 19th century. Diameter, 15½" (39.37 cm). The border is decorated with a continuous band of varied diapers. The motif of pheasants is enhanced with plum blossoms, peony blossoms, and chrysanthemums. All of the Edo period Satsuma illustrated was executed with rich and harmonious combinations of color and motif. Even those pieces decorated in the palest shades show a richness of color combinations.

46   Figure dating from the Edo period, mid-19th century. Height, 10" (25.4 cm). This figure of Kanzan unrolling a scroll is finely enameled in pale colors and gilt. Exceptionally good detail.

48   Figure dating from the Edo period, third quarter of the 19th century. Height, 3½" (8.89 cm). This figure of Jurojin is finely enameled and detailed in iron red, gosu (blue), black, turquoise, and gilt. It is marked Genzan.

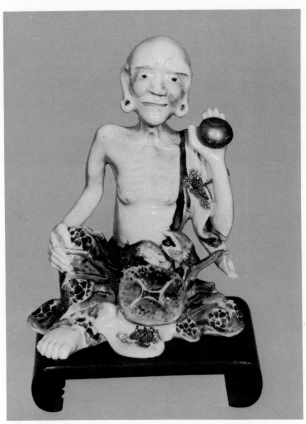

49 *Figure dating from the Edo period, c. 1860. Height, 5¼" (13.33 cm). This rakan, depicted as an emaciated elder, is finely detailed and enameled in colors and gilt.*

50 *Figure dating from the Edo period, c. 1860. Height, 3¾" (9.252 cm). Finely detailed figure is enameled in colors and gilt. The base is marked Satsuma yaki.*

51 *Figure dating from the Edo period, c. 1865. Depiction of Fukurokuju is finely detailed and enameled in iron red, gosu (blue), turquoise, and gilt. It is marked Satsuma/Genzan.*

52 *Figure dating from the Edo period, c. 1860-1865. This figure of Ebisu is finely enameled and detailed in iron red, gosu (blue), and turquoise, with extensive use of gilt. It is marked Satsuma/Genzan.*

53   *Figure dating from the Edo period, c. 1850. An important specimen in the form of Kannon, it bears the seal of Gyokuzan (art name—Chin Ju Kan, the present generation of which is still working in Kagoshima). Specimens with an authentic Gyokuzan seal are very rare. This figure of Kannon is finely enameled and detailed in iron red and gosu (blue), with black and turquoise and extensive use of gilt. This objet d'art is 7¼" high (18.415 cm).*

54   *Figure dating from the Meiji period, c. 1868. Height, 3¾" (9.525 cm). This figure of Daikoku is finely enameled and detailed in iron red, gosu (blue), turquoise, black, and gilt. It is marked Satsuma/Genzan.*

55   *Figure dating from the Edo period, c. 1865. Height, 5¼" (13.335 cm). This figure of a student is finely enameled and detailed in colors and gilt. The garb has an overall motif of various diapers.*

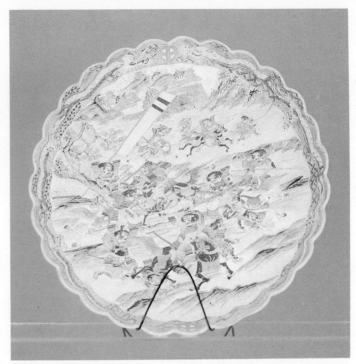

57   Charger dating from the Edo period, c. 1850. Diameter, 12½"
(31.75 cm). The central motif is referred to as "one thousand warriors."
The scalloped, fluted border is decorated with nishikide diapers and
dragons.

56   Vase dating from the Edo period, c. 1860. Height, 7¼" (19.05
cm). Broad oviform with a short neck and everted rim, it is painted in
colors and gilt. The motif features peony blossoms and foliage with bamboo and plovers. The neck and base trim are diapers with a band of mons
above the shoulder. One of a pair, it is unmarked but likely the work of
Chikusai.

58   Bowl dating from the Edo period, c. 1850. Diameter, 8" (20.32
cm). The exterior is entirely covered in gosu (blue) with gilt diapers. The
interior motif features Buddha, rakan, and Kannon enameled in pale hues
and gilt with extremely fine detailing.

59   Plate dating from the Edo period, c. 1850.
Diameter, 9½" (24.13 cm). The border of
nishikide diapers contains two dragons and the
Shimazu mon. This fluted, scalloped plate has a
central motif of rakan (without halos) finely enameled in pale hues and gilt. Base is marked Satsuma
yaki.

60   Jar with cover dating from Edo period, c. 1850-1865.
Height, 7¼" (18.415 cm). The silver (gin) cover has a gold wash
and appliques of silver chrysanthemums and foliage, with a central
reserve of a silver applique featuring maru mitsu aoi. Standing on
three legs, and bordered with an upper band of chrysanthemums
and scrolls, it has a motif of rakan finely enameled in iron red, gosu
(blue), turquoise, and gilt. The base bears the gosu (blue) mon of
the Shimazu family.

4 Satsuma Wares

Satsuma is a term synonymous with a well-known and long admired form of Japanese ceramics. To the Western connoisseur, it has come to mean a faience covered with a fine glaze possessing a beautiful network of crackles with ornamentations of varying colored enamels.

Near the close of the Momoyama period (1574-1603), Shimazu Yoshihiro, the daimyo of Satsuma province, and whose family were the overseers of Osumi province, mounted an attack against Korea as a prelude to the conquest of the Chinese Empire. In 1592, the first invasion was launched, with the second coming four years later in 1596. After several years of fighting and some strong victories, the Japanese armies were summoned back to their homeland by shogun Hideyoshi, then the military dictator of Japan.

Shimazu Yoshihiro returned to his homeland and brought with him a number of Koreans, among whom were approximately seventeen to twenty skilled potters. At first the Korean potters were settled in three villages: Kushikino, Ichiku, and Sanno gawa. According to past published works, the Korean potter named Hochiu urged his fellow craftsmen to repay their captors for the benefits they had received by introducing their art of ceramics to them.

Thus, the Korean potters were divided into two groups. Hochiu (Kwa) and some comrades relocated in Chosa, Osumi province. The second group, headed by Boku Hei (Hae) resettled in and around Naeshiragawa in Satsuma province. Both Osumi and Satsuma provinces now comprise the area of Kagoshima prefecture.

It is important to remember this division and relocation of the Korean potters in order to maintain a better understanding of the variations among Satsuma yaki. It is also important to remember that the pottery industry from its infancy up to the time of the Meiji restoration was under the patronage of the daimyo, and the daimyo was its sole support.

As for the various schools, certain individual master potters were under the patronage of the shogun and the Imperial court.

The earliest Satsuma wares (of both Osumi and Satsuma provinces) were styled after Korean prototypes. These wares were in red or red brown paste which was covered with a colorless, transparent glaze. The only ornamentation used at first was Mishima.

The Shimazu clan were collectors, and among their treasures were Chinese ceramics. It is reasonable to assume that such works were offered to the potters of this patronage for study. This class of wares would have been a revelation to the Korean potters, and could explain the great innovations and creativity of their later wares as compared to that produced by them while residing in Korea or immediately following their resettling in Japan.

Ko Satsuma yaki production included articles for use in Cha no yu. Such articles were generally small in size. The grandiose scale of objects such as palace vases and palace urns were, for the most part, objects made for Western export. Such productions did not come until the end of the Edo period (c. 1860). Ko Satsuma yaki (ko = early, yaki = ware) is termed by this writer-collector as "early period wares."

There were many varieties of Ko Satsuma yaki which would not be accepted as "refined" by Western standards. To the connoisseur of Japanese ceramics, such wares are highly prized and sought after. Among the best known of the early period wares are the following:

Jakatsu-gusuri (also known as dragon scale, reptile and/or scorpion glaze), which has a dark ground with gray and/or white glazing which possesses globules which resemble dragon or serpent scales.

Facsimiles of Sawankalok (Thai) wares, with designs executed in brown.

Mishima-Satsuma wares having overall motifs, incised into the biscuit, which were filled with white slip and glazed over. Such wares were styled after Korean prototypes.

Kuro-gusuri — monochrome black wares having a hue that falls between Chinese famille noire and Chinese mirror black. A variation of kuro-gusuri was flecked with gold dust.

Shiro-gusuri — Satsuma wares having a milk white or brownish white glaze. (See Figs. 2, 3, 4, 36.)

Monochromes — Satsuma monochromes of the early period included apple green, yellow, and tea green. Tea green is a form which had several variations including pear skin and/or russet brown glaze over the tea green. Another variation was a mixture of tea green, white, brown, and gray.

Bekko — tortoiseshell glaze.

Flambe (namako-gusuri) — Satsuma yaki of this type had a flambé (transmutation) glaze of bluish green.

Tessha-gusuri — a form similar to Chinese iron rust.

Tea green variations — brown glaze with deep green and/or black, having splashings of black and/or golden brown, and/or tea leaf, which can be flecked with gold dust. (See Fig. 1.)

All the aforementioned varieties, though not easily recognizable by Westerners, are classified as Satsuma, as were all the productions of all the kilns of Satsuma and Osumi provinces.

Up until 1787, for the most part, Satsuma wares were not decorated in the manner so easily recognizable today. To think that all Satsuma wares were void of any form of enameled ornamentation until the start of the Kwansei era would be an invalid assumption. One must realize that the ceramists working for the Shimazu family were under the patronage of one of the wealthiest families in Japan and that the daimyo was himself a patron of the arts. Therefore, it is reasonable to assume that every conceivable advantage was bestowed upon those artisans working for the daimyo.

Ko Satsuma yaki was ornamented from time to time prior to 1787. Generally, such ornamentation was limited to a monochrome, either gosu blue or iron oxide (brown), with the latter used more frequently in sketchy, pencil-like motifs, and both being used singly in scenic motifs as well. (Fig. 3 is an excellent example of gosu [blue] monochrome ornamentation.)

It was not until the Kwansei era (1787-1800) that a full range of colors, including gold, was employed for the first time. Either just prior to, or at the start of the Kwansei era, two artisans, Hoshiyama Chiubei and Kawa Yagoro, were sent by the daimyo on a journey designed as a learning experience.

The two artisans visited workshops in Hizen, Higo, Chikuzen, and Chikugo. They spent time in Seto where they observed the production of Mifukai yaki. It was at the last stop, in the Awata district of Kyoto, that the methods employed for enameling faience were learned, as well as the processes used in the production of Raku yaki (for use in Cha no yu). In the 17th century, c. 1650, several ceramists from the Awata district visited the kilns in Satsuma province, hence the intercourse of the two areas was reciprocal and would account for the close affiliation between the two wares with regard to paste, glaze, crackle, coloring, and motif.

Motifs used on middle period Satsuma wares (1787-1868) were for the most part simple, graceful, elegant interpretations of nature. Designs included florals, birds, insects, and animals, used singularly or in combinations. The employment of figures in the form of rakan, processionals, warriors, demons, et al, was not initiated and incorporated into motifs until the end of the Edo period, c. 1850-1860.

There are distinguishable variances between the wares of Satsuma province and that of Osumi province. Haku ji yaki (Satsuma whiteware) was a product of the kilns in Satsuma province. These kilns included that of Naeshiragawa. Haku ji yaki has a fine, hard grained paste, and articles were generally covered with a glaze that produced a fine network of minute crackles. The crackles are so fine that at times they can only be observed with the use of magnifying glass. Haku ji yaki was generally ornamented with simple motifs executed is soft, gentle enamels outlined in either gold or black. (See Figs. 30, 31.)

By comparison, the Satsuma wares of Osumi province, including the kilns at Chosa, tend to have a body tint that shades toward buff, with very defined crackles. The motifs were similar to the whitewares; however, the enamels employed were bold and brilliant. Motifs were generally enhanced with bold gold outlining, and, unlike the whitewares (haku ji yaki) which have fleeting gold dust sprinkled about the motif, the wares of Osumi have gold jeweling which highlights and enhances the decoration. Thus, the Osumi wares are bold in appearance and the Satsuma wares are more subdued. (See Fig. 20.)

What is the charm which has justly placed the old Satsuma yaki at the head of all Japanese faience? The question was well answered by Messrs. Audsley and Bowes *(The Keramic Arts of Japan)* when they said, ''In the entire range of keramic art there has been no surface produced more refined in treatment or more perfectly adapted to receive and enhance the value of coloured decorations than that presented by the best specimens of old Satsuma faience.''

The variance in the crackle on the wares of Osumi and Satsuma are due to the way in which the body and glaze perform in the kiln. Not being perfectly homogeneous, the glaze contracts, thus forming the lines which are referred to as "crackles." Crackles can be controlled, provided the ceramist knows how certain glazes will contract on a particular body at specified oven temperatures. The crackle is the first and probably the most important characteristic of Satsuma wares.

The network of crackles, be it delicately close or defined and large, enhances the article by producing a play of light on its surface. This is true of pieces which are undecorated as well as decorated.

On the early and middle period wares, the ceramists for the most part were careful not to hide or cover up the entire ground, unless such was specifically ordered or requested by the daimyo. Only on the modern period wares do we find the entire ground completely concealed either with monochrome or polychrome enamels. This guise was used by some producers to hide imperfections in the paste, glaze, or overall condition of the body.

The hues on the middle period wares included crimson (indian red); gosu (a hue which can appear as blue black, blue gray, or deep blue green and which is akin to prussian blue); turquoise; and pale green with black, white, and gilt. Hues which are termed halftones, such as pink, lavender, etc., were not perfected until the Tempo era (1830-1843). Color is an excellent aid for the collector and interested party to use when making an age evaluation. The hue gosu (blue) was used prior to c. 1870-1872, at which time the use of oxidized cobalt blue was initiated. Cobalt blue is a color which ranges from sapphire blue to blue violet. It was first used in Arita in 1869, one year before Dr. G. Wagner, a technical advisor from Germany working for the Japanese government, developed the art of "decoration under the glaze as applied to faience." Under his guidance the Japanese developed modern factory equipment, coal burning kilns, plaster molds, and European glazes.

Word should be mentioned of the middle period wares which have silver lids or covers. Silver (gin) has been used by the Japanese since ancient times. Until the Edo period, silver was not used by nobles or daimyos. However, during the Edo period, silver came to be used extensively in the decorative arts. Silver lids and covers found on Edo period Satsuma are generally pierced or have appliques which feature chrysanthemums (sixteen petaled), paulownia blossoms, or maru mitsu aoi (asarum). These represent the mon of the Imperial court and the Tokugawa shogun. (See Figs. 20, 22.)

The contours and sizes of the middle period wares generally harmonize with the motif. Forms include sake bottles, koros, kogos, hanna ike, ewers, wine pots, teapots, tea bowls, small bowls and dishes, as well as ornaments for Tokonoma.

It was shortly before the end of the Edo period that the so-called imitation Satsuma wares made their appearance. At the London International Exposition in 1862, Satsuma was displayed for the first time in a Western country. This was followed by displays in Paris in 1867, Vienna in 1873, and at the Philadelphia Centennial in 1876. From its first appearance in the West, Satsuma was extremely well received and greatly sought after. The so-called imitation wares were made in order to fill this overwhelming demand. The so-called imitation wares are, to the layman, hardly distinguishable from the productions of Osumi and Satsuma provinces. It is ''best'' to categorize these wares as Satsuma with a prefix indicating either the place of manufacture (the various schools), name of the potter, artist, or producer, or method or style of decoration. Among the areas (various schools) producing Satsuma wares were Kobe, Awata, Awaji, Tokyo, Kyoto, Ota, Yokohama, Wakayama, Kiyomidzu, Gojozaka, Osaka, etc.

61   Vase dating from the Edo period, c. 1860. Height, 5″ (12.7 cm). Bulbous with an elongated neck, the heart-shaped reserve features a sage in contemplation seated next to a tree. Further ornamentation includes bands of gilt diapers.

62   Vase dating from the Edo period, c. 1855-1865. Height, 14″ (35.56 cm). The shoulders are surmounted by two gosu (blue) Shi Shi. The central motif is that of rakan and their attributes. This vase is finely enameled in iron red, turquoise, gosu (blue), black, and gilt.

63   Vases (pair) dating from the Edo-Meiji period, c. 1867-1868. Height, 8¼″ (20.955 cm). These vases are molded in relief and also have moriage detailing. The theme is that of Shoki and Oni in a chase scene. Varied bands of nishikide diapers enhance the motif which is elaborately detailed in colors and gilt.

41

64   Bowl dating from the Edo period, c. 1855-1865. Diameter at widest, 16½" (41.91 cm). The motif of the eighteen Buddhist disciples (rakan) with their attributes forms the central theme. Upper and lower bands of intricate nishikide diapers capture the central theme. The base bears the gosu (blue) mon of the Shimazu family.

65   Jar with cover dating from the Meiji period, c. 1868-69. Height, 16½" (41.91 cm). The base of this jar has an unusual motif of two dragons on either side of an inscription which explains that this object was made by Chin Ju Kan, art name—Gyokuzan (see Fig. 53), in Satsuma province, in the first year of Meiji. Pieces which bear the mark of Chin Ju Kan (Gyokuzan) are rarities, regardless of the generation, and especially if dating prior to 1900. The body is molded in relief and finely enameled in blue, iron red, colors, and a lavish amount of gilt. The motif is of rakan, Kannon, and dragon against a scenic background. There is some question in the author's mind as to the authenticity of the cover. It appears to have been made at a later date, but is professional in every aspect, right down to the precisely matching colors. Due to the rarity of this object, with or without the original cover, the value has not diminished. This author is of the opinion that another jar would be next to impossible to locate.

66   Vase dating from the Edo period, c. 1865. Height, 8½" (21.59 cm). The contour reflects the Korean influence on Japanese pottery. A most attractive object, it has an upper border of butterflies in upright and inverted positions. The foot trim has a band of scrolling diapers. The glaze has a golden crackle and is rather thick. The central theme is that of a phoenix and clouds enameled in iron red, gosu (blue), turquoise, and gilt with fleeting clouds of gold dust.

67 (L to R): Coffeepot dating from the Edo period, c. 1865. Height, 6" (15.24 cm). This coffeepot has a double rope handle and a chrysanthemoid lid with a border of nishikide diapers. The central motif consists of water plants. The base is decorated with the same chrysanthemoid form as the lid. Teapot dating from the Edo period, first half of the 19th century. Height, 3" (7.62 cm). The thick iridescent crackle is golden in color and tends to run quite thick around the spout and handle. The motif of seasonal flowers and foliage is executed in colors and gilt. Matching diapers in colors and gilt decorate the lid and rim. Coffeepot dating from the Edo period, c. 1865. Height, 6½" (16.51 cm). The intense hues that were used to decorate this coffeepot include turquoise, iron red, and gilt with black. The handle is a double rope with a motif of scrolls and flowers. The motif of seasonal flowers and phoenix in flight is further accentuated with sprinkled gold dust. At one time, this coffeepot actually was used as a coffee server, and there is some staining in the paste. Such does not deter from the overall value.

68 Miniature vases dating from the Edo period, c. 1840. Height, 3¾" (9.525 cm). A pleasing design finely enameled in colors and gilt. Pairs dating from the Edo period are rarities, especially when in miniature form.

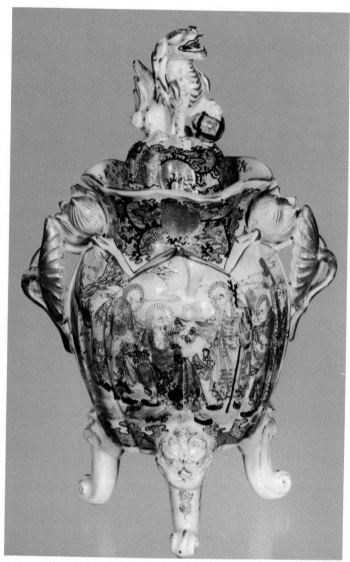

69   *Koro (incense burner) dating from the Edo period, c. 1860. Height, 12" (30.48 cm). This is a fine example of Kyoto School Satsuma-Edo period. The finial is a spray of lotus blossoms and foliage executed in pale green and pink and highlighted with gilt. The central motif of men gathering tea leaves is finely detailed. The slight irregularity in contour is due to the method of hand potting used in creating this object.*

70   *Jar with cover dating from the Edo period, c. 1860. Height, 15" (38.1 cm). The cover is surmounted by a gilt Shi Shi and tama. The contour is that of a lotus blossom with the handles formed by open and closed lotus blossoms. This jar stands on three masked, curled legs. The motif on one side is of Rakan and the reverse has a motif of scholars and students. The trim on the upper portion of the body matches the ornamentation on the cover. The interior of the rim has a scrolling gilt motif.*

71 (L): *Vase dating from the Edo period, c. 1865. Height, 7½" (19.05 cm). This vase supported by three children has a pleasing motif of seasonal flowers executed in pale shades with gilt accents. The interior of the mouth contains a scrolling motif executed in gilt. (R): Vase dating from the Edo period, c. 1860-1865. Height, 6" (15.24 cm). Similar to the vase on the left, this object has masked ears with loop (handles) and two reserves on its neck, each depicting an elder. The overall motif of leaves is executed in gilt. The three children supporting this vase have more colorful garb than those on the left. The interior of the neck also has a motif of scrolls executed in gilt.*

72 (L): *Melon-ribbed box, Edo period, c. 1865. Diameter, 5" (12.7 cm). (R): Melon-ribbed box, Edo period, c. 1865. Diameter, 4" (10.16 cm). Both objects are decorated with seasonal flowers, foliage, cloud formations, and butterflies in colors and gilt. The interior of each lid is ornamented with polychrome butterflies and gilt speckles.*

73   Cha wan (tea bowl) dating from the Edo period, first half of the 19th century. Diameter, 3¼" (8.255 cm). The glaze is thick with a golden iridescence. The ornamentation consists of a single spray of flowers and buds with foliage. In the latter part of the 19th century and early 20th century, similar glazes were reproduced. However, the coloring indicative to the Edo period was not, and it is this difference that invariably gives away age and authenticity.

74   Vase dating from the Edo period, c. 1850-1860. Height, 6" (15.24 cm). This vase has a rather bulbous body, gilt rope trim around the neck and paulownias and scrolls at the base. The motif which is minutely detailed is finely executed in intense hues with extensive use of gilt. In some areas the motif stands away from the body due to the extreme thickness of some of the enamels, especially where rockwork, grasses, and foliage are denoted.

75   Kogo (box) dating from the Edo period, c. 1860. Length, approximately 2½" (6.35 cm). This kogo is enameled in washes of only three shades, turquoise, iron red, and brown, with black accents.

46

76 *Kogo (box) dating from the Edo period, c. 1865. Diameter, 3" (7.62 cm). The exterior of this kogo is enameled in gosu (blue) with raised gilt ornamentation. The reserve on the lid has a scenic motif of a governess and children on a picnic.*

77 *Vase dating from the Edo period, c. 1860. Height, 9½" (24.13 cm). This vase has two reserves. The one illustrated is filled with pheasants among flowers and foliage. The reserve on the reverse contains a depiction of children playing go and drinking tea. The overall motifs of clouds and phoenix form diapers throughout. The interior of the mouth is decorated with cherry blossoms and foliage. With extensive gilt throughout, it still maintains a subtle and rather subdued character.*

78 *Vase dating from the Edo period, c. 1860. Height, 25" (63.5 cm). Kara Shi Shi handles (ears) with tama. The Shi Shi at the right is the female. Depicted on one side are two samurai warriors at the end of battle. The reverse has a full-length portrait of Benten. Intricately detailed diapers form a delicate pattern of butterflies around the neck. Enamels include "silver."*

47

79 *(L to R) Top row: All of the pieces in this photograph date from the Edo period, c. 1865. Pair of vases on stands having slightly bulbous bodies and slightly flared trumpet necks, height, 13½" (34.29 cm), ornamented with motif of birds and flowers in colors and gilt. Vase with animal head ears, decorated with floral sprays in colors and gilt, and ornamented with gilt pheasants, height, 12" (30.48 cm). Pair of vases on stands, elephant head handles, cylindrical bodies, ornamented with floral motifs and birds, with nishikide diapered borders. Height, 16" (40.64 cm). Vase, bulbous body, slightly flared trumpet neck, nishikide diapered bands throughout, with central motif of floral designs executed in colors and gilt. Height, 13" (33.02 cm). Bottom row: Pair of vases with sprigged on floral motif consisting of prunus blossoms and enameled in colors and gilt. Height, 6" (15.24 cm). Koro (incense burner) on tripod stand, surmounted with Kara Shi Shi with tama, having border of nishikide diapers and a central motif of floral sprays executed in the Kutani palette. Height, 11" (27.94 cm). Vase, cylindrical form with open work, decorated with floral motif of seasonal flowers and fleeting clouds of gold dust. Height, 5½" (13.97 cm). Koro (incense burner) with interesting ornamentation. The handles are Daikoku's magical hammer. The motif of seasonal flowers is bordered by nishikide diapers, overall execution in colors and gilt. The trim of rope and tassels adds an additional touch to this piece which stands 10" high (25.4 cm). Vase with globular body having a motif of seasonal flowers, a top band of nishikide diapers executed in colors and gilt. Height, 5" (12.7 cm).*

5 Potting and Decoration

The contour of an object was determined by its intended use. There were a variety of methods employed in the creation of such an object.

The potter's wheel has been in use in Japan since prehistoric times. The potter's wheel is a horizontal disk which revolves on a vertical spindle which holds the clay being shaped by the potter. The shaping of the clay is completed by the control of the potter's hands, with respect to the wet clay, and the movement of the wheel. Objects made with the potter's wheel are termed "thrown." Pieces potted in this manner will have concentric circles on the base. These lines are termed "ito guri." The Korean method of removal (a majority of the early and middle period wares were produced by Korean potters) was to cut the object from the sum of clay with a thread, from left to right. This may be discerned by examining the base of a given object.

Mechanical Devices

Jolley — A convex mold placed on the wheel to form the interior contour of dishes and plates.

Jigger — A hollow mold used in the same manner as the jolley for forming the exterior contours of cups and bowls. A sum of clay would be placed in the rotating mold and forced into the required contour with a plunger.

Hollow Molds

A mold is a cavity formed of clay, wood, and, for modern productions, plaster of paris. The clay would be pressed by hand onto the exterior or interior of the hollow mold, thus forming the contour. Hollow molds were also used to form various parts of an object which were later luted together with slip. A modern

---

Opposite Page

80   (L to R) Top row: All pieces date from the end of the Edo period. All are Kyoto School Satsuma. Covered jars, produced by Taizan and decorated in Tokyo (blanks sent to Tokyo for decoration). The motif of plum blossoms and trees (ume) with bamboo is executed in pale shades with diapered borders. Height to top of lid, 7¼" (18.415 cm). Vase with conventional ornamentation of flowers and birds produced by Taizan and sent to Tokyo as a blank. Height, 11¾" (29.845 cm). Vases (hanna ike) made by Kozan, decorated with farm scene of boy and cow, enameled in colors and gilt, with lower border band of nishikide diapers. Height, 11" (27.94 cm). Vases (pair) produced by Kozan having a motif of monkeys in relief hanging from branches in relief. Enameled in colors with extensive use of gilt, they stand 15" high (38.1 cm). Bottom row: Figure of bijin dressed in ordinary attire and painted in colors and gilt. Height, 10¼" (26.035 cm). Vases (pair) attributed to Taizan, with motif of bamboo and birds enameled in shades of green, brown, and gray with gilt accents. Height, 11" (27.94 cm). Figure of a man dressed in ordinary garb, painted in colors and gilt. Height, 9½" (24.13 cm). Bottles (pair), attributed to Kozan, decorated with floral motifs in colors and gilt. Height, 12" (30.48 cm). Figure of court attendant with garb decorated with colors and extensive gilt accents. The clothing is decorated with intricate diapers resembling patterns found on silk brocade. Height, 13½" (34.29 cm).

49

method for producing articles is termed ''casting,'' in which liquefied clay (slip) is poured into a porous plaster mold. The plaster absorbs the water and gradually the coating turns into solid clay.

Hand Potting

- A sum of clay would be manipulated by hand, pulling it and pushing it into the required contour. A spatula was used to smooth the object into a more refined shape. Most pieces potted in this manner have a foot trim which was gouged from the base. This is discerned by examining the base and finding a coiled or swirled effect in the paste.

- Forming the clay into long ropes or coils, which were then wound around to form the wall of an object was another method employed in hand potting. The coils would generally be smoothed with a spatula or by hand. Objects potted in this manner usually have an applied foot trim (a coil of clay which was luted onto the base).

- The least used of the hand potting methods (with regard to Satsuma) was beating in which a mallet was used to beat the clay into the required contour.

Relief Decorations

Relief decorations appear to be greatly admired by Western collectors. The various forms of relief decoration and application were difficult to achieve due to the need for a constant temperature within the kiln. Objects decorated with moriage motifs had to be exposed to the direct action of the kiln, and if the temperature were not constant (if it fluctuated even slightly), it caused the enamel to boil.

Moriage (to pile up) consists of applied slip (clay) decoration in which the motif was formed by hand and applied to the biscuit. Such motifs may be glazed, unglazed, enameled, or left in the natural state. (See Fig. 87.)

Slip-trailed motifs were formed by trailing liquefied clay (slip) through a tube onto the biscuit. The technique is akin to the method used in decorating a cake.

En gobe is a term applied to white or colored slip used to form motifs or applied as a support for a glaze or enamel. (See Fig. 41.)

Warabide (also termed pâté sur pâté) motifs are generally applied in high relief and take on the form of a fern and scroll motif.

Pâté sur pâté means paste on paste.

Hakeme motifs are created by reducing the clay (slip) to a liquefied state so that it can be applied by brush.

Mishima motifs were incised or impressed into the biscuit with a stamp or dye. The impressed or incised motifs would then be filled with either slip or enamel, and such are usually found in low relief.

Molded in relief motifs rise from the surface of an object and were formed by cutting or carving a particular motif into the hollow mold.

Mezzo relievo motifs were cut from the wall of an object. Such motifs are generally scenic and have projecting detail and high elevations within the motif. (See Fig. 42.)

Sprigged on (sprigging) motifs were formed by hand or with the use of a hollow mold, and then were applied to an article by luting.

The following is an excerpt from a paper written by Sir Ernest Swatow.[1]

In February of last year (1877) I had the opportunity of visiting the Korean village of Tsuboya, where I was most hospitably lodged and entertained by one of the inhabitants, to whose care I had been specially commended by a Japanese friend. There is nothing distinctive in the appearance of the people or in the architecture of their houses to attract the notice of a passing traveler; they all speak their native tongue, and wear Japanese dress; Tsuboya is in fact just like any other village. The principal potteries belonging to the Koreans are situated on the side of a hill to the south of a high road, together with the kilns belonging to the Tamamoyama Kaisha, a company recently started by some Kagoshima Samurai. The Tsuboya crackle is produced at this establishment and at another on the opposite side of the road owned by a Korean named Chin Ju Kan, but most villagers devoted themselves to the manufacture of common brown earthenware. The principle of the division of labor seems to be throughly well understood and applied by these workmen. One will confine himself, for instance, to the bodies of teapots, of which he can produce 150 in a day; another makes the lids, a third the spouts, a fourth the ''ears'' or projecting pieces into which the handle is inserted, and to a fifth is assigned the joining of these parts together. Generally the members of a family work in concert, and form a sort of co-operative society, which is joint owner of a kiln with other such societies. The clay used for the coarse ware is found at Isakuda and Kanno gawa, near Ichiku, and at Terawaki, Kukino, and Noda, near Iju-in, all in the neighborhood of Tsuboya. Chocolate-colored, red, and green glaze are obtained from Tomua, Kammuri-take, and Sasa-no-dan, while Ishiki furnishes the glaze for water jars and other large articles of this coarse ware. Three sizes of wheel

---

1. Sir Ernest Swatow, British Minister in Peking. The excerpt was taken from a paper prepared and read by Sir Ernest before the Asiatic Society of Japan.

are in use, the smallest of which is formed of two wooden disks about 3 inches thick, the upper one being 15 inches, the lower 18 inches in diameter, connected by four perpendicular bars somewhat over seven inches long. It is poised on the top of a spindle planted in a hole of sufficient depth, which passes through a hole in the lower disk and enters a socket in the under side of the upper disk, and the potter, sitting on the edge of the hole, turns the wheel round with his left foot. The largest wheel is about twice the size in every way of the smallest.

The kilns are built up the face of a hill in parallel rows. Each is divided into a number of chambers with openings in the intervening partitions to allow for the passage of flame and hot air from the lower end of the kiln right up to the head, and there are apertures in the side of every compartment, a larger one for the ware to be passed in and out by, which is of course closed during the firing, and a smaller one through which the workmen in charge can watch the progress of the baking. The fuel is placed in the lowest chamber, which is about six feet square, and consists of split pine logs about two feet in length and a couple of inches in diameter. Two hundred and fifty or sixty bundles of wood are required for a single firing, which usually lasts about thirty six hours. No stands are used for the brown earthenware while it is being baked, but the articles are piled on each other, every second one being upside down; they consequently adhere together slightly when brought out of the kiln, but a slight tap with a piece of wood is sufficient to separate them. Between the heavier pieces, such as large jars used for packing tea, small bits of dry clay are inserted to keep them apart. The glaze is put on by immersion, the article, as for instance a teapot, is dipped into the liquid upside down, in such a manner that very little gets inside, and then being quickly reversed, is set on its base, so that the glaze flows down pretty equally all around. When dry the glaze is of a yellowish-gray opaque color, and it is put on before the article is subject to any process of firing.

The material used for the finer kind of earthenware, that is, saishiki-de or painted ware, and nishiki-de, into the decoration of which gold enters as well as colors, consists of white clay from three localities, namely, Mount Kirishima, Ibusuki, and the gold mine at Yamagano, of white stone from Kaseda and Kushiki, and of white sand from Kominato. Ibusuki supplies in addition a second kind of clay, called bara, which is said to be very brittle, and no doubt is the ingredient which gives somewhat of the character of porcelain to certain pieces of the ware. The Kaseda stone is used also for glazing when powdered and mixed with the ashes of nara wood *(Quercus glandulifera),* or some other sort of hard timber.

The clay and stone are well pounded, soaked in water, and passed several times through a fine sieve placed over a receiver. The minute particles which settle at the bottom are then taken up and dried on boards. To this process is given the name midzu-boshi, or water-drying, and it is common to all branches of manufacture. For the fine white earthenware four kinds of clay, together with bara and white Kaseda sand, which have been previously subjected to midzu-boshi, are mixed in certain proportions known to the experienced workmen. Lumps of this stuff are placed upon wooden blocks, and pounded with hammers to the extent of about three thousand blows, by which it is brought into the state of raw material; but, previously to being actually converted into clay for the potter's use, it requires about three thousand more blows. It is considered to improve in quality the longer it is kept.

The kilns in which nishiki-de and saishiki-de are baked are one-celled, and built of clay upon a foundation of brick, with walls about six Japanese inches thick. Fire is kindled in the mouth of a passage which projects from the front of the kiln, and the hot air passes up this to the chamber, where it can circulate freely round the muffle, in which the biscuit is deposited. The largest of these kilns have the following dimensions:

EXTERNALLY	INTERNALLY
Height 5.5 feet (Japanese measure)	Height 4.5 feet
Diameter 4.5 feet	Diameter 3.5 feet
Height of hot-air passage 5.0 feet	Height of hot-air passage 1.2 feet
Width . . . . 0.9 feet	

A space of four inches in width is left between the muffle and the inner wall of the kiln. For nishiki-de three firings are necessary; first the su-yaki, after which the glaze is put on; secondly, the honyaki, after which the piece is painted and gilded; and thirdly, slow and gradual firing, which develops the colors; the durations being twenty-four, forty-eight, and ten hours respectively. During the last firing the temperature is observed from time to time through an aperture near the top, the test employed being a piece of pottery marked with various pigments which gradually assume the desired tints as the heat increases.

A memorandum drawn up by an official of the Kagoshima prefecture, for presentation to the Commission which presided over the Industrial Exhibition held last autumn in Yedo, gives the composition of the pigments used for producing the various colors of the fine Satsuma wares. Dr. Edward Divers, F.R.S., Professor of Chemistry at the Imperial College of Engineering, has kindly examined specimens of these materials in Yedo, and has furnished me with their English names. The mixtures for the various colors are as follows:

Red — ground white glass, soft or lead variety (shiratame no ko); white lead (to no tsuchi); colcothat or red oxide of iron (beni-gara), and silicious earth called binoka tsuchi.
Green — ground white glass; white lead, copper oxychloride (roku-shyo), and silicious earth.
Yellow — ground white glass, red lead (komeitan), silicious earth, and metallic antimony (toshirome).
White — ground white glass, silicious earth, and white lead.
Blue — ground glass and smalt (a ground blue glass, the color of which is due to a cobalt compound, the Japanese name is bana konjyo).
Purple — ground white glass, white lead, and manganese.
Black — ground white glass, white lead, an earthy manganese ore containing a little cobalt (wensei), and a very silicious carbonate of copper, apparently ground and elutriated malachite (sbionuki-roku shyo).

At the pottery belonging to Chin Ju Kan,[1] I saw a group being modelled in white clay, which after baking and glazing assumes a light cream crackle. These articles were intended to be decorated later on with gilding and colors. The potters here possessed only two old pieces of plain ware, a choji-buro and a figure of a child playing with a diminutive puppy. The choji-buro is a utensil formerly of two pieces, namely, a brazier and a boiler on the top of it, and is intended for distilling oil of cloves, though in practice it is used merely as an ornament. The artists were employed in modelling figures of

---

1. Chin Ju Kan (art name, Gyokuzan), one of the most famous of the Satsuma potters.

Kwan-on and Dharma in white clay, with the conventional face and robes given to Buddhist personages, and toes are all of the same length. A third was engaged upon a tiger, sitting up in a cat-like posture, intended to be two and a half Japanese feet in height when finished. Most of their figures are modelled from drawings in Indian ink, but the colored designs are laid on from memory. Until fourteen years ago a ware called Bekko-yaki was made at this village, the colors of which were intended to imitate tortoise shell. It was a common ware, and used to be exported to Nagasaki in large quantities. A piece of this, said to be old, which was exhibited to me, had green blotches, as well as the two usual colors, yellow and brown.

At the Tamanoyama Company's establishment all sorts of ware are produced, common brown pottery, inferior blue-and-white, and highly gaudy crackle. Here I found a workman engaged in modelling a statuette of Christ after a sentimental woodcut in a religious periodical called the ''Christian Observer''; he had copied the face and beard with considerable accuracy, but had draped the body and limbs in the robes of a Buddhist priest. Some stoves of brown earthenware, imitated from American iron stoves, were already ready for the kiln; their price was to be seven dollars delivered in Yedo. I saw also some huge white vases of monstrous shape, composed of hexagons, circles, squares, piled up as it were pell-mell, the result of an attempt at originality, unhampered by traditional notions of form.

This account given of themselves by the Korai jin (as they are called) is that all the inhabitants of the village, peasants as well as potters, are descended from Koreans brought over during the period Keiho (1596-1610) by a Satsuma samurai named Ijuin. Until about three years ago they wore their hair tied up in a knot at the top of the head, but most of them now wear the Japanese queue, or cut their hair in the style which has been introduced from abroad. They informed me that in former days they dressed themselves in their own costume on special occasions, as for instance when they went forth to salute the daimyo of Satsuma as he passed through their village on his way up to Yedo. One of the potters was good enough to put on this dress in order to give me an idea of the appearance which they presented. The knowledge of the Korean language is still kept up by some among them, whose duty it is to interpret between castaway Korean junkmen and the Japanese officials. It appears that these people marry freely amongst themselves, identity of surname not being considered an obstacle as it is in China, but seldom intermarry with Japanese, except they be a member of the samurai class.

81 *Koro (incense burner), attributed to Taizan, dating from the end of the Edo period. Height, 8¼" (20.955 cm). The overall ornamentation of chrysanthemums and paulownias with scrolls executed in gosu (blue), iron red, turquoise, and gilt. Animal head ears add an interesting ornamentation. This objet d'art stands upon an inverted bowl (Awata Satsuma), which was supposedly exhibited at the Vienna Exhibition held in 1873, thus dating this bowl c. 1870-72. Although potted in Kyoto (the Awata district), it was sent to Tokyo for decoration and purportedly was painted by Hoyen Matsumoto. The diameter at the widest is 12¼" (31.115 cm). The motif is quite intricate indicating it was painted in Tokyo. It contains mythical and realistic sea creatures including the octopus, dragon, and other sea animals, some of which are dressed in elaborate garb and carrying spears. It is finely enameled in rich colors and gilt.*

82 *(L to R): Vases (pair) dating from the end of the Edo period. Height, 21½" (54.61 cm). These vases are richly and boldly decorated with a motif of flowers, foliage, and birds in a conventional style. The enamels include gosu (blue), iron red, turquoise, white, black, and gilt. The neck and foot trim are ornamented with nishikide diapers and chrysanthemums and scrolls. Charger dating from the end of the Edo period. Diameter, 18" (45.72 cm). The central theme of a Ho-o (phoenix) is rather bold in both depiction and coloring. Finely enameled, the overall coloring consists of gosu (blue), iron red, turquoise, black, and gilt. The border contains nishikide diapers in geometric forms.*

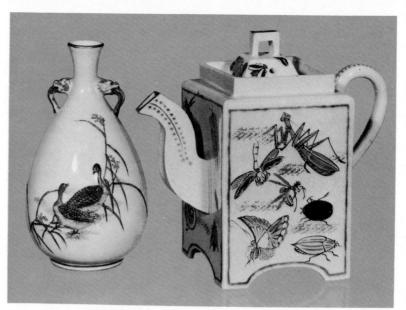

84   (L) Vase dating from the Meiji period, c. 1875. Height, 4½" (11.43 cm). Modified pear shape with animal head handles, with moriage motif of quails among grasses. The fine enameling is quite realistic with just a hint of gilt accents. (R) Teapot dating from the Meiji period, c. 1871. Height, 5" (12.7 cm). The interesting motif consists of varying insects including beetles, moths, butterflies, praying mantis, snails, etc. Carefully enameled in colors including gosu (blue), turquoise, shades of green, lavender, and gilt. It is signed Kinkozan.

83   Vase dating from the Meiji period, c. 1871-1872. Height, 15" (38.1 cm). This vase is decorated in two shades of gosu (blue) with extensive gilt accents and black detailing. Depicted are warriors in battle. Victorian in form, and likely made for export to the West. It bears the signature of Kinkozan.

85   (L to R) Top row: Tea set dating from the Meiji period, c. 1885. Overall height of each piece, 4½" (11.43 cm). Signed Kinkozan, this set has a motif of flying cranes and bamboo finials. Bottom row: Box dating from the Edo period, c. 1810. Diameter, 5" (12.7 cm). It is decorated with floral sprays and butterflies in pale hues with just a hint of gilt. Teapot dating from the Edo period, c. 1800. Height, 4½" (11.43 cm). Kame finial and finely enameled in pale hues with a motif of peony blossoms. Pitcher dating from the Edo period, c. 1840. Height, 4½" (11.43 cm). Enameled in pale hues with a motif of peaches and chrysanthemums (Kinkozan).

86 *Brush pot dating from the Edo period, c. 1865. Height, 3½" (8.89 cm). The overall motif is that of water plants and foliage with sprinkled gold dust throughout. The piece is rather light in weight. Signed Kinkozan.*

87 *Vases (pair) dating from the Meiji period, c. 1870-1875. Height, 9½" (24.13 cm). The vases are of the Tokyo School and have moriage motifs which were formed and applied by hand. The motifs have a pale celadon glaze and the overall execution is finely detailed and enhanced with gilt. There is additional ornamentation in the form of a horse's head and loose ring handles. There are two inscriptions on the bases. One reads: "Made in Great Japan, in the abundant pottery garden/ Shiba District" (Tokyo). The other is a potter's seal which reads "Seishi."*

88 *Covered jar dating from the Meiji period, c. 1872. Height, 4¾" (12.065 cm). A rare combination of Totai Shippo (ceramic bodied cloisonné) on Satsuma. This piece is signed Kinkozan. The entire body is decorated in geometric diapers, plum blossoms, maple leaves, and bats. The two reserves, which feature flowers, foliage, and birds, are decorated in Awata Satsuma style (Kinkozan).*

89 *(L) Bottle dating from the Meiji period, c. 1890. Height, 5" (12.7 cm). The motif of feudal lords is set in a scenic depiction with extensive use of red orange and gilt with gilt jeweling. (R) Bottle dating from the Meiji period, c. 1890. Height, 7½" (19.05 cm). The motif is similar to the bottle on the left. Use of diapers is more predominant on this specimen that that on the left.*

90   Covered jar dating from the Meiji
period, c. 1885. Height, 7½" (19.05 cm).
Standing on three masked feet, this jar has a
Kara Shi Shi finial and two winged dragon ears.
The motif is pleasing and consists of students
with scholars and students on the reverse. The
enamels are vibrant and there is extensive use
of gilt. The entire depiction is bordered with
nishikide diapers.

92   Tea caddy (oversized) dating from the Meiji period, c. 1885. Height, 14" (35.56 cm). The
overall motif of a family is heavily gilded and finely detailed. There is an inner lid which has a motif
of gilt scrolling.

91   Bottle-vase dating from the Meiji
period, c. 1905. Height, 3¾" (9.525 cm).
Bordered by a top and bottom band of
millefleur, the center band contains Karako
playing blindman's bluff. Signed Jozan.

93   Jardiniere (base) dating from the Meiji period, c. 1880 (Kyoto School). Height, 12". Diameter, 12" (30.48 cm). The overall motif is of intricately executed nishikide diapers. Each of the three panels has a ringed rope and tassel motif. The interior of each panel is enameled with irises, peonies, and chrysanthemums.

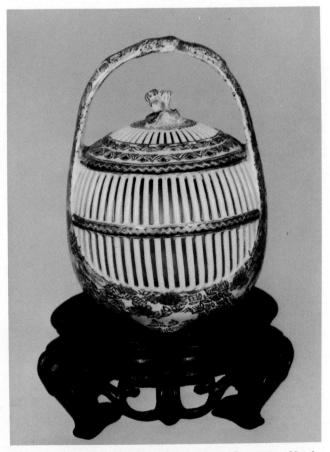

94   Vases dating from the Meiji period, c. 1910. Height, 9" (22.86 cm). These vases have a pleasing contour which includes a slightly elongated and flared trumpet neck and mouth. The motif is of alternating bands of millefleur and nishikide diapers with scenic reserves featuring samurai and villagers.

95   Cricket cage dating from the Meiji period, c. 1900. Height, 3¼" (8.255 cm). The reticulated cage has a finial comprised of kiku buds. The finely enameled overall motif is that of diapers and chrysanthemoid forms.

59

96   *Vase dating from the Meiji period, c. 1880-1885. Height, 3¾" (9.525 cm). The side illustrated shows a scene with two children at play. The reverse has a panel filled with peony blossoms. Side panels are filled with nishikide diapers and overall gilt accents.*

97   *Ewers dating from the Meiji period, c. 1895. Height, 13" (33.02 cm). The lids have Kara Shi Shi finials and a motif of nishikide diapers. The swirling designs from the base to the neck represent the essence of aroma rising. Well-contoured, with chainlike formations from the base to the spout, the iron red-orange bodies have reserves filled with flowers and foliage and scattered motifs of maple leaves with extensive gilt highlights. These are excellent examples of Awata Satsuma.*

98   *Vase dating from the Meiji period, c. 1880-1885. Height, 2½"
(6.35 cm). A beautiful miniature with extensive gilt accents on brown
borders (top and bottom), with side panels of mons and nishikide diapers.
The reserve illustrated features children and a scholar in minute detail.
The reverse features a reserve filled with delicately detailed peony
blossoms and foliage.*

99   *Saki pitcher dating from the Meiji period, c. 1885-1900. Height,
4½" (11.43 cm). Standing on three bracket feet, this saki pitcher has a
lower border of panels featuring nishikide diapers. Intermingling with
the diapers are reserves of circular medallions filled with various family
scenes. This is bordered with the pattern of one thousand butterflies.
The central theme, above, is a continuous winter scene with cloud formations of gold specks. The spout and handle have gilt scrolling motifs.
The lid missing, the owner had an ivory lid made to fit this piece which
is attributed to Yabu Meizan.*

100   *Vase dating from the Meiji period, c. 1900. Height, 3¾" (9.525
cm). The central motif is that of a street scene featuring an outdoor market.
Signed Suzan.*

61

6 The Awaji School

Awaji School Satsuma is so named after the island of Awaji, where the wares were produced. Kashu Mimpei (1796-1871) was a potter. Sometime around 1818, he first began to devote himself to the art of ceramics. Between 1830 and 1840, with the help of a Kyoto ceramist, Ogata Shuhei, he was able to develop a pottery closely resembling that produced in the Awata district of Kyoto. The Awaji wares are similar in paste to that of Awata, but, in general, the enamels used were of paler hues and were generally transparent. The outlining of motifs was most often executed in black. The body tint of Awaji Satsuma is a bit more cream-colored than that of Awata and is covered with a fine network of crackle which was produced with a fine glaze. The Awaji School also made wares similar to Bekko yaki. Following Mimpei, the business was carried on by Kashu Sampei. (See Fig. 17.)

101   *Jar with cover dating from the Meiji period, c. 1885-1900. Height, 16" (40.64 cm). Kara Shi Shi finial with tama, Shishi handles, and three mask feet add to the ornamentation of this covered jar. The motif of feudal lords with scenic background is surrounded by bands and panels filled with nishikide diapers and extensive gilt accents.*

102   *Figure dating from the Meiji period, c. 1885. Height, 15" (38.1 cm). This rakan (Chota Panthaka) is finely detailed and enameled in shades of the Kutani palette with turquoise accents and gilt. The robe is ornamented with motifs incorporating diapers, flowers, dragons, tigers, and phoenix. The Rakan is seated upon or resting next to a tree, depending on interpretation.*

103   *Bowl dating from the Meiji period, c. 1885. Diameter, 8½" (21.59 cm). Decorated in iron red-orange, gilt, and turquoise, the side illustrated depicts a family scene, and the reverse has a scenic motif with lords and children. Features extensive use of gilt with upper and lower borders of nishikide diapers.*

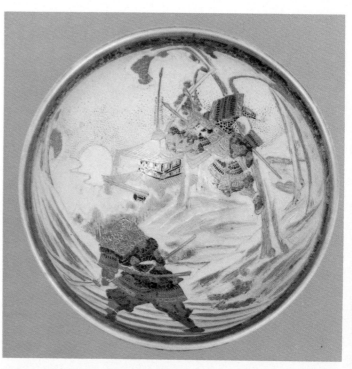

104   Bowl dating from the Meiji period, c. 1885. Diameter, 5" (12.7 cm). The interior features two rakan and a child against a scenic background. The border contains nishikide diapers. The exterior is decorated with turquoise paulownia blossoms with gilt leaves.

105   Bowl dating from the Meiji period, c. 1890. Diameter, 4½" (11.43 cm). The exterior has alternating mons and paulownia blossoms. The interior is a battle scene between two samurai. There is a small interior band at the rim which contains a diaper. It should be noted that the interior motif takes place during the winter, as the ground is covered with snow.

106   Shell-shaped bowl dating from the Meiji period, c. 1884. Diameter, 7" (17.78 cm). This shell is supported by three clam-shaped feet. The interior is a motif closely associated with Kinkozan wares: flowers, foliage, and flying cranes executed in colors and gilt.

107　Vase dating from the Meiji period, c. 1895. Height, 16″ (40.64 cm). Hexagonal form, the alternating panels depict a family scene and flowers with foliage.

108　Bowl dating from the Meiji period, c. 1885. Diameter, 6½″ (15.875 cm). Lotus form, the interior of this bowl contains a scene of a family on a balcony-terrace with a view of a lake and waterfall. The overall motif is completely decorated with nishikide diapers. The border features alternating panels of pink and blue grounds filled with flowers. The exterior contains mons and diaper motifs.

109　Saki pitcher dating from the Meiji period, c. 1895. Height, 3″ (7.62 cm). Pear-shaped with gilt trim on spout and handle, it has three bands separated by small bands of gilt design on a black ground. The lowest band contains a motif of Sanju rokkasen. The center band contains various No masks. The upper band contains karako. This piece bears the mark Shunzan in seal form.

110 *Vase dating from the Meiji period, c. 1900. Height, 3½" (8.89 cm). Bulbous and standing on three legs, the central motif is of karako astride flying phoenix birds. The upper bands of nishikide diapers form a lappet border. This piece is marked Hozan.*

111 *Vase dating from the Meiji period, c. 1885. Height, 3½" (8.89 cm). Double gourd shape has a base with alternating reserves filled with karako. The overall motifs of nishikide diapers and flowers are executed in shades of green, yellow, red orange, and gilt. This vase bears the mark Shozan.*

112 *Bottle-vase dating from the Meiji period, c. 1885. Height, 4¾" (12.065 cm). Upper and lower bands of nishikide diapers, with the lower consisting of geometric forms only, frame the central motif of a performance of a No drama. The hues are vibrant and intense, with extensive use of gilt. This piece bears the Eizan mark.*

113   *Bowl dating from the Meiji period, c. 1880. Diameter, 4½" (10.795 cm). The interior of this bowl contains seventy-seven figures in a scene showing a processional entering a temple. The exterior has panels with excerpts from the interior motif.*

114   *Bottle-vase dating from the Meiji period, c. 1900. Height, 3½" (8.89 cm). The motif in the upper band has a rendition of Benten. The lower panels have scenes showing samurai riding into battle. The bands are separated by diapers, mons, floral reserves, and the eight treasures.*

115   *Vase dating from the Meiji period, c. 1895. Height, 3¼" (8.255 cm). Overall motif of gilt mons and scrolls with the elongated neck decorated with nishikide and gilt diapers. There are two circular reserves. The one pictured features an archer with his attendant.*

116   *Koro (incense burner) dating from the Meiji period, c. 1890. Height, 4" (10.16 cm). Square form, with animal head ears, the entire body and lid are decorated with nishikide diapers. Two finely enameled panels feature karako at play and a daimyo and his consort. The costumes are finely detailed with diapers, and the ground is speckled with gilt.*

117   *Tea set dating from the Meiji period, c. 1900. The motif of a No mask (Okina) and lacquered box (takamakie) are finely detailed and enameled in colors and gilt.*

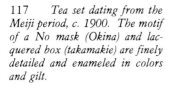

118   *Vases dating from the Meiji period, c. 1885. Height, 3¼" (8.255 cm). Upper and lower bands of nishikide diapers with a central motif of heart-shaped reserves featuring family scenes, karako, one thousand butterflies and nishikide diapers are all finely enameled in colors and gilt. There is gilt jeweling throughout, and surrounding the reserves are gilt speckles.*

119   *(L): Koro (incense burner) dating from the Meiji period, c. 1880. This koro stands on three stub feet and is ornamented with loop handles and a sprig finial. The pierced lid has a treatment of nishikide diapers overall. The continuous motif features bijin and children. This piece is signed Hozan. (R): Teapot dating from the Meiji period, c. 1885. Height, 3½" (8.89 cm). Overall nishikide diapers, with a lappet upper border surrounding two heart-shaped reserves, each of which features students and a scholar.*

120   *Pitcher dating from the Meiji period, c. 1880. Height, 26" (66.04 cm). Reminiscent of Victorian styling, this object is covered in blue monochrome and has extensive gilt highlights. Each side has reticulated gilt medallion and what could be termed a motif of English roses and foliage. (Awata School.)*

7 The Kyoto School

Readers' note: This area of discussion is limited to Satsuma wares, Kyoto School; therefore, no mention is made of artists such as Rokubei, Ninsei, Kenzan, et al. It is important to remember the intercourse of information between Satsuma artisans and the ceramists of Kyoto (especially the Awata district). The Kyoto ceramists learned the techniques of enameling faience long before such was employed in the same manner by the artisans of Satsuma and Osumi.

For the most part, there is little variation in the quality of the paste, the techniques, and the methods of decorating when comparisons are made between the productions of Satsuma and that of the Kyoto School (middle period wares). For the layman, the productions of Satsuma and Kyoto are hardly distinguishable, one from the other. The most obvious difference is in the body tint. Kyoto Satsuma wares tend to be a bit more yellowy. Middle period Satsuma wares of the Kyoto School were decorated with fewer hues and more neutral tones than those of the modern period. Modern period wares were decorated with a kaleidoscope of mingling colors and with extensive gilding.

Perhaps the most important line of potters was the Kagiya family, more commonly known as "Kinkozan." This line of potters worked from the 17th century up until 1927. The name Kinkozan was not used until 1756, when the head of the family, Kobayashi Kihei, was appointed "official potter" to the Tokugawa shogunate from which the title was bestowed. This first generation of the Kinkozan line (third generation of the Kagiya family) supplied the shogunate with articles for us in Cha no yu.

Generations

First — Kagiya Tokuemon worked up to 1693.
Second — No records exist.
Third — Kobayashi Kihei (Kinkozan I) established the family business.
Fourth — Kobayashi Kihei (Kinkozan II) worked in the late 18th century.
Fifth — Kobayashi Kihei (Kinkozan III) worked in the early 19th century and turned out the wares which we identify as middle period Kinkozan Awata Satsuma/Kyoto School.

Sixth — Kobayashi Sobei (Kinkozan IV) sometime between 1872 and 1877 began exporting to the West. He employed many potters and decorated and pro—duced little by his own hand.

Seventh — Kobayashi Sobei (Kinkozan V) worked up to 1927. He too employed a number of workers and made wares for Western export.

Of all the Kyoto School (Satsuma) ceramists, it was the Kinkozan line that is associated with cloisonne on pottery (Totai Shippo). An object having a pottery body covered with a fine glaze possessing a network of fine crackles, having metal cloisons, and an enameled motif executed in the style associated with Satsuma wares is properly termed ''Cloisonne on Satsuma.'' (See Fig. 88.) It was the sixth generation of the Kagiya family — Kinkozan IV (Kobayashi Sobei), who initiated the production of the aforementioned wares, sometime between 1872 and 1877. For a short time these wares were popular in Western markets. However, the wares were not able to withstand much handling and often hairlines (spiders) formed in the pottery bodies. These wares were decorated with soft enamels which did not respond to the polishing processes, thus resulting in dullness. On the whole, Totai Shippo (pottery bodied) was not comparable, either in appearance and stamina, with the metal bodied cloisonne wares which were becoming popular in Western markets. At the end of the 19th century, c. 1895, this line of production was discontinued. Due to their short-lived appearance, values for these wares, as well as demand, are quite high.

In general, middle period Kinkozan Satsuma wares had a body tint of yellowy cream which is much admired for its softness in appearance. Motifs were interpretations of nature and the enamels employed included crimson, green, purple, yellow, pink, blue (used sparingly), and black and white with gilt accents. Motifs generally had subdued gold outlining and were highlighted with fleeting gilt cloud formations. (See Fig. 32.)

Modern period wares (up to 1927) are also much admired. The workers employed by S. Kinkozan from 1900 to 1927 were aptly skilled at producing minute (almost microscopic) motifs having great detail. Although many connoisseurs find such wares lacking in artistic interpretation, as compared to middle period wares, one must admire the stamina required to labor for so many hours in order to produce these objects. (See Fig. 166.)

Just as important as the Kinkozan line, is that of Taizan. The name Taizan was not used until the second generation adopted it as an ideograph for Obiya, the name of the family business. The following list shows the various generations of the Taizan family. Note that all but the first generation used the name Taizan Yohei.

Generations

First — Tokuro worked from 1675 to 1711 and produced Raku yaki.

Second — Taizan Yohei I worked from 1716 to 1735 and adopted the name "Taizan."

Third — Taizan Yohei II distinguished for his use of Mazarine blue, c. 1755.

Fourth — Taizan Yohei III produced utensils for use in Cha no yu and worked until 1800.

Fifth — Taizan Yohei IV appointed as potter to the Imperial court and produced wares for Imperial use from 1801-1820.

Sixth — Taizan Yohei V produced faience for the Imperial family from 1830-1843. (See Fig. 35.)

Seventh — Taizan Yohei VI worked to 1853.

Eighth — Taizan Yohei VII worked to c. 1875.

Ninth — Taizan Yohei VIII produced wares in the same styles as his contemporary, Kinkozan V. Some of these wares were executed with moriage decorated motifs, as were those produced by Kinkozan V.

Another notable family of potters was the Hozan. There is no accurate information about the early members of the family. It was the head of the seventh generation who opened a kiln in the Awata district of Kyoto. The ninth generation was the first to use the name Hozan.

Generations

Ninth — Hozan I (Yasubei Bunzo) worked to 1723.

Tenth — Hozan II (Yasubei) worked to 1752.

Eleventh — Hozan III (Bunzo) worked to 1769.

Twelfth — Hozan IV (Kumanosuke) worked to 1797 and produced faience for the court in Edo (Tokyo).

Thirteenth — Hozan V (Yasuemon) worked to 1818.

Fourteenth — Hozan VI (Heibei) worked in the early 19th century.
Fifteenth — Hozan VII (Komanosuke) worked to 1842.
Sixteenth — Hozan VIII (Bunzo) worked to 1889.
Seventeenth — Hozan IX (Kumanosuke) worked from the turn of the century.

Hasegawa Komenosuke (art name — Bizan) is synonymous with the Kyoto School. In 1820 he joined the fourth generation of the Taizan family and worked until 1838. Bizan second generation decorated his faience wares predominately with motifs taken from the No dance drama. He worked up to 1862. Bizan third generation produced wares for Western export. In 1887, the family business was taken over by his son, the fourth generation of the Bizan line of potters.

Wares produced in districts other than Awata may also be referred to as Kyoto School. The two major centers of production other than Awata are named Kyomidzu and Gojozaka. These districts of the Western capital (Kyoto being the Western capital) produced many fine ceramists including Okumura Yasutaro (art name — Shozan); Nakamura Tatsunosuke (art name — Ryozan); and Ito Koemon (art name — Ito Tozan).

Ito Tozan worked from the turn of the century to WW II. He was a ceramist whose works displayed skills of the highest degree. His faience (produced at a factory in Gojozaka) was decorated with a wide range of hues and his execution was technically perfect. By 1910, his works had been awarded a total of ninety-five medals, won at both foreign and domestic exhibitions.

Perhaps one of the largest of the modern producers was Tanzan (Rokuro), son of Tanzan (Yoshitaro). Tanzan Yoshitaro settled in Kyoto in the Awata district in 1854. The paste of his wares had an ivory cream body tint with designs of florals and animals executed in naturalistic hues. Tanzan (Yoshitaro) also produced wares with motifs executed in slip (moriage), which were made specifically for Western export. The Tanzan family was associated with Kiri Kosho Kaisha, a company located in Tokyo, for the purpose of expediting the wares to Western markets. Among the patterns produced with slip (moriage) were arabesques and warabide in high relief, as well as lacy patterns slip-trailed in low relief.

The following, from the article "More on Kinkozan and Taizan," by this author was excerpted from *Jinrikisha Days in Japan,* E.R. Scidmore, Harper & Bros., Franklin Square, 1891, and is reprinted with permission of *The Orientalia Journal.*

The porcelains of Kyomidzu, renowned as they are throughout Japan, figure lightly in the export trade lists, as compared to the immense shipments of decorated faience from the Awata district, for which there is such demand in foreign countries. On the main street of that quarter, which is the beginning of the Tokaido, the larger establishments cluster near together, and Kinkozan, Tanzan, and Taizan attract one in turn. Latticed walls and plain gate-ways admit visitors to a succession of show-rooms, where they may wander and look. As it is the characteristic Japanese custom to consider every foreigner as a mere sight-seer, who puts tradesmen to trouble for nothing, the bushy-headed young men in their clean, cool cotton gowns make no effort to sell until he purchases something. Then he is led through further rooms to godowns or upper chambers, and their more desirable wares are displayed.

Kinkozan's specialty is the manufacture of the cream-colored faience with a crackled glaze, which, when decorated in one way, is known as Kyoto or Awata ware, and when covered with a blaze of color and gilding is the gaudily, modern, or Kyoto Satsuma, exported by the ship-loads to America, where its crude hues and cheap effects are enjoyed. No cultivated Japanese, however, would ever give these monstrosities a place in his own home. In America, these garish six-months-old vases and koros are even passed off as old Satsuma, to which softly-toned and simply decorated ware it is no more like than is a Henri Deux tazza to a Limoges garden-stool. Kinkozan turns out also a coarse shippo yaki, or cloisonne enamel, some on faience and some on copper ground; and the blue-and-white-gowned young man will lead one past garden and godown, and show one every stage and process of the manufacture of the different wares. The potters sit in little open alcoves of rooms, each with his low wheel and heap of clay before him. One old man sits with his feet doubled up before him, his right foot locked fast in the bend of the left knee, and the left foot laid sole upward on the right thigh, in the impossible attitude of so many Buddhas. This position he maintains with comfort for hours, and this lean, bald-headed, old man, wearing nothing but a loin-cloth and a pair of huge round, owlish spectacles, is as interesting as his work. He puts a handful of wet gray clay on the wheel before him, making it revolve with a dexterous touch of the hand, while he works the lump of clay into a thick, broad bowl. With his fingers and a few little sticks he soon stretches the bowl upward, narrows it for a neck, broadens and flattens it a little at the top, and presently lifts off a graceful vase and sets it on a board with a row of others. In another place the workmen are grinding and working the clay; in another, preparing the glaze and applying it, and near them are the kilns in every stage. In a further garden the decorators are at work, each with his box of brushes and colors beside him, the vase being kept in half-horizontal position before him by a wooden rest. Each piece goes from one man to another, beginning with the one who sketches the designs in faint outline, thence passing to him who does the faces, to a third who applies the red, to a fourth who touches in the diaperwork and traceries, and so on to the man who liberally bestows the gilding. Lastly, two women slowly burnish the gold by rubbing it over with wet agates or carnelian.

At the other houses faience, in an infinity of new and strange designs and extraordinary colors is seen, each less and less Japanese. All these Awata potters work almost entirely for the foreign market, and their novelties are not disclosed to the visitor, nor sold in Japan, until they have had their vogue in the New York and London markets. From those foreign centres come instructions as to shapes, colors, and designs likely to prove popular for another season, and the ceramic artists abjectly follow these foreign models. All this helps to confuse a stranger; for, though the wares are named for the districts, towns, and provinces of their supposed nativity, he finds them made everywhere else-Satsuma, in three or four places outside of Satsuma.

121   *Bottle dating from the Meiji period, c. 1900. Height, 6½" (16.51 cm). Kyoto School, and though not signed, it is attributed to Taizan. The ground is shaded from light to dark burnt orange. This bottle stands on four legs and has, at the shoulders, applied moths in relief, as well as a smaller insect surmounting the stopper. The stopper and neck have a slight band of nishikide diapers.*

122   *(L to R): Vase dating from the Meiji period, 1890. Height, 9¼" (23.495 cm). The ground is shaded from light to dark purple-lavender (a hue which seems rather rare to find on Satsuma of the Awata School). The motif of flowers and foliage is highlighted and outlined with gilt, as are the outlines of the diapers. Vase dating from the Meiji period, c. 1895. Height, 8½" (21.59 cm). The body is colored in a cross hue which appears lavender pink. The motif in a central band is that of chrysanthemum heads against a white ground accentuated with gilt jeweling. Scattered throughout are mons enameled in red, blue, and gilt on a white ground. The ears are wings with a ring and tassel trim. Pitcher dating from the Meiji period, c. 1888. This is a flat back pitcher, a style copied from Worchester (an English firm). It has a gilt handle with gilt highlights in each of the circular reserves which feature sprays of flowers and foliage. This pitcher is signed Kinkozan.*

123   (L to R) Sugar bowl dating from the end of the Edo period, c. 1865. Height, 4" (10.16 cm). Melon-ribbed, with vinelike finial, the continuous motif of tea gatherers is enameled in pale, subdued shades and slightly accentuated with gilt hints. It is signed Kinkozan. Teapot dating from the Meiji period, c. 1900. Height, 3½" (8.89 cm). Pear-shaped, it has a motif of flowers and foliage associated with Kinkozan wares. Shoe-shaped cha wan dating from the Meiji period, c. 1885. Enameled in colors and gilt with a motif of flowers and butterflies. Signed Kinkozan.

124   Miniature jar dating from the Meiji period, c. 1885. Height, 2¾" (6.985 cm). The lid is surmounted with a pierced tama. The motif is millefleur pattern in colors and gilt. Two circular reserves feature karako and flowers.

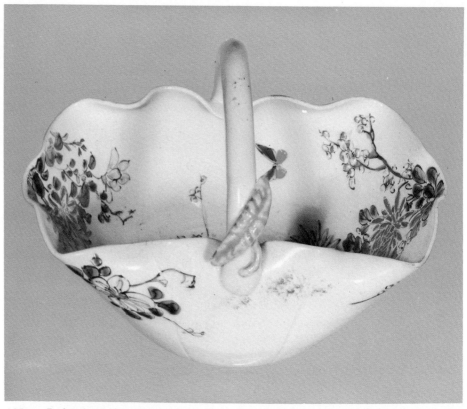

125   Basket dating from the Meiji period, c. 1895. Diameter, 6½" (16.51 cm). Overall floral motif features butterflies and flower buds applied at the base of the handle. The design is highlighted with hints of gilt. Signed Kinkozan.

126 Jar-urn with lid dating from the Meiji period, c. 1885. Height, 16½" (41.91 cm). The lid is surmounted with a chrysanthemoid form knob. The nishikide diapers are extended and continued from the lid to the neck, at which point the body becomes bulbous. The central motif of chrysanthemums was executed with the Mishima technique. The flowers and foliage lie against a yellow blue ground which ends with a band of diapers.

127 Vase dating from the Meiji period, c. 1895. Height, 17" (43.18 cm). Heavily gilded throughout, the motif of plum blossoms and birds is striking against the dark ground which shades from black at the top to a light red brown at the base. Throughout the scrolling patterns at the neck and base are chrysanthemum heads. (Note: This author has found that regardless of the number of petals, specimens which have any form of chrysanthemum tend to be pieces of better quality.)

128 Jar with cover dating from the Meiji period, c. 1895. Height, 8½" (21.59 cm). Standing on three long legs, the cover is surmounted by a gilt Kara Shi Shi. The lid is decorated with nishikide diapers and gilt alternating with circular mons. The overall motif of wisteria and maple leaves with birds and foliage lies against a muted blue ground. Gilt legs and gilt ringed ears add an interesting touch.

129   (L to R) Top row: Vases (pair) dating from the Meiji period, c. 1885. Height, 3" (7.62 cm).
The motif depicts a processional entering a temple. Vase dating from the Meiji period, c. 1900.
Height, 3½" (8.89 cm). The central motif of quails was executed in the moriage technique, applied
by brush and hand, and enameled. Signed Kinkozan. Second row: Koro (incense burner) dating
from the Meiji period, c. 1900. Height, 2½" (6.35 cm). Panels of birds and flowers against a creamy
gold ground. Signed Taizan. Covered jar dating from the Edo period, c. 1800-1820. Height, 3¾"
(9.525 cm). Now missing a cover, its owner had an ivory lid made, and the lid has heart-shaped
cutouts, thus converting this piece into an incense burner. Vase dating from the Meiji period, c.
1900. Height, 3½" (8.89 cm). The cobalt oxide and gilt ground has two panels, each featuring a
barnyard scene. Third row: Teapot dating from the Meiji period, c. 1910. Height, 2½" (6.35 cm).
Decorated with a continuous band of courtesans. Brush pot dating from the Taisho period, c. 1925.
Height, 2" (5.08 cm). Teapot dating from the Taisho period, c. 1920. Height, 1½" (3.81 cm). It is
enameled in the millefleur pattern. Fourth row: Vase dating from the Meiji period, c. 1910. Height,
5" (12.7 cm). Vase dating from the Taisho period, c. 1915. Height, 5¼" (13.335 cm).
Signed Kinkozan. Pitcher dating from the Showa period, c.1938. Height, 4½" (11.43 cm).

130   Toothpick holder dating from the Meiji period, c. 1900. Height, 4½" (11.43 cm). The back side contains the pocket for toothpicks. Figures, regardless of form, are not easily found.

131   Vase dating from the Meiji period, c. 1900. Height, 7" (17.78 cm). Signed Kinkozan, the vase is decorated in a manner similar to certain varieties of Longwy.

132   Vase and pedestal dating from the Meiji period, c. 1890-1905. Height, 36" (91.44 cm). Typical of the Art Nouveau period is this vase with matching pedestal. The vase has two bands filled with flowers in alternating shades of orange-pink and white with gilt. The vase has a central motif of irises and leaves against a blue ground. The pedestal, which has hints of stalactites of blue glaze hanging from the applied water flowers, is a marvelous mixture of molded and applied relief work. The blue is under the glaze and it ran in such a manner as to enhance the freeflowing movement of the motif.

133   *Picture frame dating from the Taisho period, c. 1914. Dimensions, 5" × 6½" (12.7 cm × 16.51 cm). The signature is obliterated, however it is attributed to Kinkozan. This frame was tacked to the wall and was made with three perforations. The picture was slipped in through a slot in the back. The motif is that of flying cranes and tortoises.*

134   *Bucket dating from the Meiji period, c. 1900. Height, 6½" (16.51 cm). The ground is muted and shades from light to medium blue. The handle and bar are decorated in gilt. The motif of morning glories and vines is enameled in white and shades of green with gilt highlights.*

135   *Saki cups dating from the Showa period, c. 1925. Diameter, 2¾" (6.985 cm). Having a gilt rim, each shows a bijin representing a different season. (Cherry blossoms in the motif on the left and maple leaves in the motif on the right.)*

136   (L to R): Salt dating from the Showa period, c. 1935. Pin tray dating from the Showa period, c. 1930. Saki pot dating from the
Showa period, c. 1934. All three specimens are decorated in millefleur pattern (one thousand flowers). The pin tray is signed Satsuma.

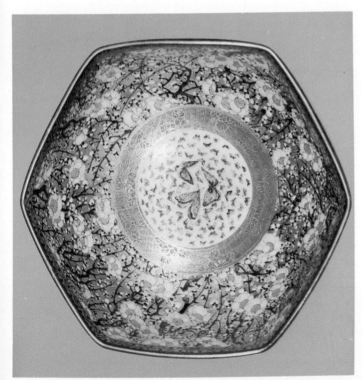

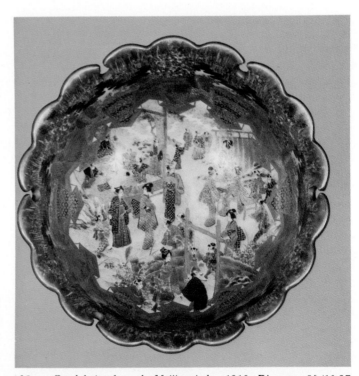

138   Bowl dating from the Meiji period, c. 1910. Diameter, 5" (13.97
cm). The foliate-scalloped rim is decorated with irises and flower gardens
against a gilt ground. The interior depicts a village scene (daily life)
executed in colors and gilt. The exterior has reserves featuring court
scenes. Signed Kinkozan.

137   Bowl dating from the Taisho period, c. 1920. Diameter, 4¾"
(12.065 cm). Hexagonal in contour, the theme throughout is of plum
blossoms and foliage against a gilt ground. The center medallion has a
motif of one thousand butterflies against a cream ground and is enameled
in colors and gilt. This bowl bears the signature Fuzan.

139   Cha wan (tea bowl) dating from the Meiji period, c. 1900. Height, 2½" (6.35 cm). The interior is decorated in colors and gilt in the millefleur pattern. The exterior is decorated in the millefleur pattern which is interspersed with black and gilt cloud formations. There are four reserves of varied contours including circular and fan-shaped. Each of these reserves (medallions) contains a scene, and the one pictured shows a scholar's desk. Signed Yozan.

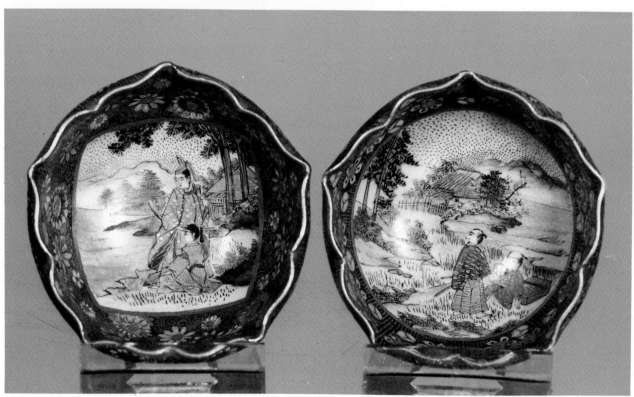

140   Master salts dating from the Taisho period, c. 1920. Diameter, 2½" (6.35 cm). The interior and exterior are finely enameled with the millefleur pattern. The interior of each contains a scenic motif featuring a lake, mountain, and figures.

8 The Tokyo School and the Moderns

Hayata Takemoto was born in 1848. Until the start of the Meiji period, he worked with Inoue Ryosai, who later produced Sumida Gawa wares. Hayata Takemoto established a kiln in Tokyo. The production included Tokyo School Satsuma wares. In 1873, at the International Industrial Exposition held in Vienna, he won first prize for a Satsuma incense burner. Hayata Takemoto is termed by this collector as the ''founder'' of the Tokyo School of Satsuma artists and potters.

For the most part, the Tokyo School was one of decorators. Large quantities of faience was sent in the blank to Tokyo for decoration. Of the modern wares, one can say the motifs for the most part were based on Buddhism, myth, and legend. Among the foremost Tokyo School motifs is that of rakan and kannon with dragon. This is especially true of the wares decorated from the turn of the century to WW II. (See Fig. 189.)

On the whole, Tokyo decorators covered the entire body of an object with vibrant mingling hues and made extensive use of black and gilt. For the most part, it appears that this was employed in order to hide imperfections and inconsistencies in both the glaze and paste. It would appear that much of the wares sent in the blank to Tokyo from Kagoshima and other areas, were perhaps wares of slightly inferior quality with regard to potting and technique. This does not mean that the execution of motifs was second rate. On the whole, the Tokyo decorators were skilled artisans. Those ceramists of the Tokyo School who produced their own pottery appear to have used more aesthetically appealing motifs, often in combination with motifs executed in slip (moriage) and highlighted with gilt. (See Fig. 87.)

Perhaps the most important modern decorator was Yabu Meizan of Osaka. At age sixty, in 1910, he was still active as an artist. However, he did employ decorators (pupils) in his studio. (See photo on page 84.) The Satsuma wares attributed to Yabu Meizan may not have always been decorated by his own hand, but the great and delicate manner of his execution of motifs and their balance with the overall contours of specific articles have not been surpassed by any other of the ''modern'' decorators. His interpretations were of the highest merit.

Among the moderns who should receive mention is Miyagawa Kozan, synonymous with the Makudzu kiln of Ota, Yokohama. The ninth of the Makudzu potters, Kozan was seventy years old in 1910, and at that age he was still actively producing faience. He was an artist of the Imperial court and was honored with a ''green ribboned medal.'' His son, Hanzan, was also a potter of great skill. In 1879 a factory was established in Yokohama (Ota), and Miyagawa Kozan was invited to work at this establishment. The factory was originally suggested by a vassal of the Shimazu family; hence the connection with Satsuma wares from the start. Materials for the production of Kozan's faience were secured from Kagoshima and Kyoto. Many of his 19th century wares were molded in high relief.

After the turn of the century, the ceramists of Satsuma (Kagoshima prefecture) not only continued to produce pieces comparable to middle period wares, but a new development was added. Masataro Keida of Kagoshima was the foremost potter of the prefecture after the turn of the century (c. 1905). He continued production of his wares, styled after middle period wares, but added delicately pierced motifs, beautifully executed. The only comparison that can be made between the pierced works of the moderns is to compare such to Hirado porcelain wares. It would appear to this writer-collector that porcelain would be a much better medium for such execution of design. Another potter producing works of this kind was Chin Ju Kan (art name — Gyokuzan), and the present generation is still working.

Other of the modern Kagoshima potters include Togo Jusho, Sameshima Kunseki, Kumamoto Kinji, and Uyeno Yachiro.

142   Koro (incense burner) dating from the Meiji period, c. 1910. Height, 3½" (8.89 cm). Standing on long tapered legs, this koro has an intricate network of geometric diapers executed in red, blue, and gilt, throughout. The diapers are interspersed with heart- and diamond-shaped medallions, each of which depicts a scene of courtesans strolling through paths lined with cherry trees in full bloom. There are two masked animal ears and a spire finial.

141   Koro (incense burner) dating from the Showa period, c. 1928-1934. Height, 3¼" (8.255 cm). The motif of rakan and dragon is one which was used extensively during the Showa period (prior to WW II). This miniature stands on three curled legs. The base is entwined with a dragon molded in relief. The lid is surmounted with a Shi Shi. The motif is basically gilt, black, and red brown with black and white accents. There are small scenic medallions scattered throughout the body and base along with a cross and circle (mon) in gold.

143   Koro (incense burner) dating from the Meiji period, c. 1900. Height, 4½" (10.795 cm). The domed cover is surmounted with a crouching rabbit. The central motif is that of alternating medallions and panels featuring karako at play, scenic motifs, floral sprays, and one thousand butterflies.

144   Koro (incense burner) dating from the Meiji period, c. 1900. Height, 2½" (6.35 cm). The body is covered in cobalt blue with raised, gilt, five-petaled flowers and scrolls overall. There are two panels featuring a governess and children against a background of flowers and grasses. The base bears the signature Taizan.

145   Koro (incense burner) dating from the Meiji period, c. 1895. Height, 5½" (13.97 cm). Square form standing on four angular feet, with lid bearing a flat knob finial. The gilt motif of the lid consists of cloud formations filled with gilt diapers and overall motifs of gilt flower heads. The upper and lower bands have a gilt diaper. The shoulder is enameled with the same motif as the lid. There are two themes, and that pictured shows part of an eight-fold screen (two folds are not visible—one on each side). The backside has a motif consisting of a screen enameled with wisteria and foliage. The base has an unusual Kinkozan marking.

146   Koro (incense burner) dating from the Meiji period, late 19th century, c. 1900. Height, 4" (10.16 cm). Now missing its original pierced cover, this koro is still an excellent example of the pierced openwork associated with certain varieties of Satsuma made at the turn of the century. The only decoration is the molded pattern (bands) above and around the pierced motifs (the style so often associated with Hirado porcelains). The overall effect is enhanced with elephant head handles and masked feet.

147   Kogo (box) dating from the Meiji period, c. 1910. Diameter, 2¾" (6.985 cm). The disk form body is enameled on one side with a panel depicting women and children washing clothing at the riverside. The second panel features a garden scene. The overall ground is cobalt blue with gilt flower heads, scrolls, and diapers. This kogo is marked Kinkozan.

148   Koro (incense burner) dating from the Meiji period, c. 1910. Height, 2" (5.08 cm). Standing on three splayed feet and having animal head ears, this piece features two panels depicting a woman and two children. The ground is turquoise with gilt diapers.

149   Wine pot dating from the Meiji-Taisho period, c. 1915. Height, 7½" (19.05 cm). A blank sent to Tokyo for decoration, the motif is that of rakan and a dragon against scenic vignettes. The base has several markings including Choshuzan, Satsuma Kuni (Satsuma province, but not referring to the decoration). The ammonite shell pattern is found on the lid and upper portion of the neck. A coiled dragon forms the handle and spout.

150   Cricket cage dating from the Meiji period, c. 1905. Height, 5" (12.7 cm). Standing on four squat feet, the motif of flower gardens and bijin is continuous throughout the handle and down the side panels and features a river scene at the front and back centers. The band encircling the rim has medallions of flower heads in colors and gilt. The cover is surmounted with a flower head in gilt. Signed Kinkozan.

151   Tea set dating from the Meiji period, c. 1910. Each piece has a band of nishikide diapers. The central motif of chrysanthemums and foliage was executed in shades of yellow and brown with gilt accents.

152   (L to R) Coffeepot dating from the Taisho period, c. 1920. The ground is cobalt blue with gilt accents (somewhat worn), with gilt handle, spout, and finial. There are two panels featuring seated bijin and wisteria. This specimen bears the mark Hododa. Teapot, dating from the Showa period, c. 1926-1927. The overall motif is bamboo executed in green and black. The handle is in the form of a twig and is ornamented with gilt flower heads and scrolls, as is the spout. Signed Kinkozan.

153   *Vase-bottle dating from the Taisho period, c. 1920. Height, 5" (12.7 cm). Decorated with two panels featuring rakan whose garb is ornamented with nishikide diapers on a gilt-speckled ground. The panels are framed by borders of nishikide diapers and these borders are framed with wide panels of millefleur. Marked Dai Ni Hon with a gold cross and circle and Hododa.*

154   *Vase dating from the Taisho period, c. 1920. Height, 4¾" (12.065 cm). Similar to the specimen in the preceding photograph, it differs in contour, but markings are identical.*

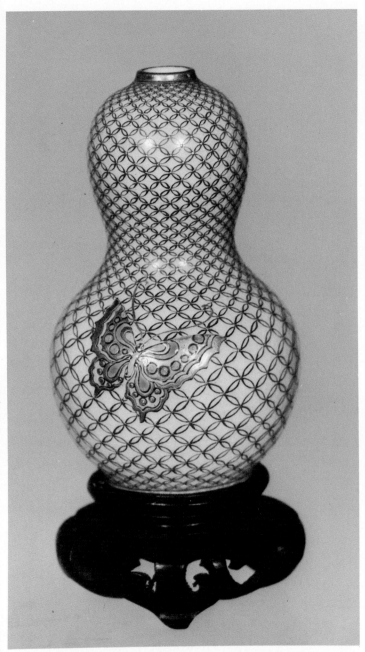

156   *Bowl dating from the Taisho period, c. 1923. Diameter, 4¾"
(12.065 cm). The motif depicts three children seated and likely playing a board game. The scalloped rim has a gilt crosshatch motif against
a red brown ground. The exterior is decorated with flower heads.
Signed Kinkozan.*

155   *Vase dating from the Meiji period, c. 1900. Height, 2¼" (5.715
cm). The overall motif of diapers in red monochrome is reduced in size
near the waist of the double gourd form. The diaper is enlarged as it covers
the lower portion of this miniature, and it decreases in size as the motif
approaches the neck. The diaper known as "Shippo tsunagi" (joined
circles) is common and appears within a group of diaper patterns but is
seldom found singularly. The sole ornamentation apart from the diaper is a
butterfly enameled in turquoise, lavender, and gilt.*

157   *Bowl dating from the Taisho period, c. 1920. Diameter, 4¾"
(12.065 cm). Decorated overall with the millefleur pattern in
polychrome and gilt, the interior contains three reserves. The fan-
shaped center reserve features women and karako. The two outer
reserves feature a riverscape with waterfowl, foliage, and a cherry tree
blossoming. Signed Hozan.*

91

158   Bowl dating from the Meiji period, c. 1910. Diameter, 3¾"
(9.525 cm). Hexagonal in form, the ground is cobalt blue with gilt lotus
scrolls overall. The interior features a circular medallion enameled in
polychrome and gilt on a gilt speckled ground. Signed Shuzan.

159   Bowl dating from the Showa period, c. 1930. Diameter, 7"
(17.78 cm). Having a scalloped rim, the interior features four reserves,
the largest depicting a family beside a riverbank. The smallest reserve
depicts five seated rakan. The other two reserves show elders and feudal
lords. The exterior is decorated with flower heads. A gilt cross and circle
(mon) is on the base.

160   Vase dating from the Taisho period, c. 1925. Height, 2¼"
(5.715 cm). The overall motif is termed one thousand butterflies. On this
particular specimen the motif is executed in red, blue, and black with gilt
outlines. Signed Hatori.

9 *Satsuma Decorated Blanks*

The advent of World War I (1914) brought to a halt the production of European hard-paste porcelain, and the supply on hand was quickly depleted. Another source of supply had to be found, namely Japan. During the war years (1914-1918), Japanese porcelains, mostly in European styles, were exported in large quantities. During these same years, undecorated Satsuma blanks were exported as well, but in lesser quantities. The majority of the blanks were exported between 1918 and 1928. There are, however, existing examples of decorated Satsuma blanks which date prior to 1918 and after 1928.

The hobbyist approach of decorating porcelain blanks during the latter part of the 19th century seems to apply to the Satsuma blanks, with the exception of those pieces decorated by the Pickard Studios of Chicago. In 1917 Pickard decorated a variety of Satsuma blanks with a standard motif referred to as "Bouquet Satsuma." This design was awarded a gold medal at the Panama Pacific Expositon.

With the exception of Pickard decorated blanks, the individual artists who decorated these wares were not connected with wholesale or retail outlets. Of the privately decorated blanks, very few were ever sold on the open market.

The decorating process was slow and never achieved the popularity of hand-painted chinawares. Satsuma is a soft glaze ware, and a majority of the decorators achieved the best result by using over-the-glaze soft enamels which differ from the enamels used on porcelain. The enameling process was tedious. Within the range of soft enamels, varying hues fire at different temperatures. The wider the range of colors used, the more times an article had to be returned to the kiln. (E.g.: Red fires at a higher temperature than black.) The blanks were exported with the glaze already fired. Thus the minimum number of firings would be two plus the one in which the glaze was fired. Great care had to be taken so as not to disturb this glaze. For example: black could not be fired more than twice or it would flake off taking the glaze with it. To add to the slowness of decorating, shading for visual effect was time-consuming and required great expertise.

The decorators of Satsuma blanks were innovative. Many artists experimented with lustre interiors and overall, flat monochrome finishes. During the 1918-1928 period, the use of lustre (orange and orange gold) was predominant on certain classes of Japanese export porcelains. Pearlized lustre was more predominant during the 1930s. The use of orange gold lustre lent a Tiffany effect to the decorated blanks. Those pieces which have a flat monochrome interior finish are reminiscent of the European green used on certain classes of Chinese export wares. Some of the decorators were quite inventive and imaginative. They experimented with techniques which were at times used by the Japanese during the Meiji period in order to give the appearance of age and authenticity to some productions of faience. These techniques included the immersion of the blanks into boiling tea in an attempt to define and darken the crackle. The majority of blanks examined by this collector are decorated with raised enamels. (Enamels are thick and have varying degrees of relief.)

During the years from 1918 to 1928 styles were in transition. This transitional expression is reflected on the decorated blanks. Motifs range from Art Nouveau to combinations of Art Nouveau and Art Deco to pure Art Deco (also known as Art Modern). Designs can be formal, semigeometric, or a combination of the two. Common denominators include the use of black outlining and a gold, jewel-like enamel. The artists seemed to instinctively cover foot trims, interiors of spouts, neck rims, bottoms of legs, etc., with either black or gold enamel.

There appear to be two schools of design — ''East Coast'' and ''West Coast.'' Although the techniques employed by both schools are basically the same, there are extreme variances in the end result. East Coast artists tended to be conservative (formal). For the most part designs were more conventional. Partiality was shown to pastel shades such as pink, blue, yellow, lilac, and green, used in combination with black and gold. West Coast artists displayed exceptional flair. Their motifs were usually flamboyant and intricate. Shading was used to its maximum, with objects often showing a magnificent blend of several hues. Perhaps the best examples of the West Coast School are the specimens illustrated and attributed to Annie Cleveland, artist from the Northwest.

Identifying marks can be found on decorated Satsuma blanks. The blanks can be marked with the country of origin (either Nippon or Japan, depending upon the year of manufacture or export). Unmarked pieces were likely affixed with a paper label (see Marks Section). Occasionally one comes across a decorated blank which is artist signed, or even dated. More often the decorated blanks have nothing more than the artist's initials.

Satsuma blanks decorated by American artists and amateurs, as well as the Pickard Studios, have been overlooked in the past. Often collectors and interested parties confuse these wares with American Art Pottery. Until recently there was a lack of information as well. After one gets over the initial shock that these wares are not "Japanese in the truest sense," one can find them aesthetically appealing in their own right.

Satsuma decorated blanks are a newly acknowledged collectible, therefore price trends and values have been recently established. The trend appears to be equivalent to prices and values as applied to Satsuma wares decorated in Japan. One must remember that playing an important role in the trend of values and market prices is rarity. Although not terribly old (collectible rather than antique) these objets d'art do not have high availability. This rarity would tend to push the prices and values higher at a fast pace, as more collectors become acquainted with this category of Satsuma.

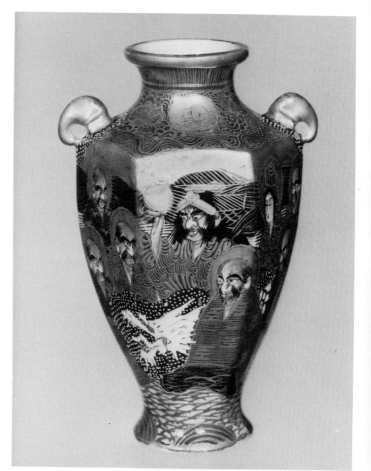

161 *Vase dating from the Taisho period, c. 1920. Height, 2¼"
(5.715 cm). A modified double gourd, the motif (a variation of Shippo
bishi-cloisonné in a diamond pattern) increases in size as it approaches the
base and diminishes in size as it approaches the pinched waist. The motif
has an upper and lower band of black and gilt scrolls. The diaper is
executed in red, yellow, blue, and gilt.*

162 *Vase dating from the Taisho-Showa period, c. 1925-1928.
Height, 4½" (11.43 cm). The motif of rakan and dragon is quite common. Execution of the motif is quite good and basically black, red, brown,
and extensive gilding, including two gilt elephant head ears. The base has
a gold cross and circle (mon) and markings which read Dai Nihon Satsuma
yaki.*

163 *Vases (pair) dating from the Meiji
period, c. 1910. Height, 11½" (29.21 cm).
Hexagonal in form, the ground is cobalt
blue with gilt flowers and scrolls. Featured
are two panels depicting bijin and attendants on a veranda overlooking a lakeside
scene.*

96

164   Vases (pair) dating from the Taisho-Showa period, c. 1926. Height, 1¾" (4.445 cm). Cobalt blue ground with gilt flower heads (somewhat worn due to handling). Featured are two panels with scenic backgrounds and a mother with child in colors and gilt. The backside has a panel which is filled with floral sprays.

165   Vases (pair) dating from the Showa period, c. 1935. Height, 2¼" (5.715 cm). Featured are heart-shaped panels depicting a family scene and rectangular panels depicting a family scene. The side panels and border contain flower heads and maple leaves in colors on a gilt ground.

97

166 *Vases (pair) dating from the Meiji period, c. 1910. Motif is a continuous scene of karako at play. The upper border is in millefleur in polychrome with bands of diapers in gilt on black and red grounds. Signed Shuzan.*

167 *Vases (pair) dating from the Taisho period, c. 1918. Height, 3½" (8.89 cm). The upper and lower bands are of millefleur in polychrome and gilt on a gilt ground followed by bands of gilt cross-hatched pattern on a black ground. Featured are two panels, one depicting warriors, the other women and children. Markings include Dai Nihon Satsuma Denzan sei.*

169   *Toothpick holder dating from the Taisho period, c. 1920. Height, 2¼" (5.715 cm). Standing on three square feet, the cylindrical toothpick has an upper border band of half choji hana bishi (cloves in a flower-shaped diamond pattern) in gilt on a black ground. The oval medallions are filled with karako enameled in polychrome on a gilt speckled ground. The ground surrounding the medallions is decorated with the millefleur pattern. Signed Kinkozan.*

168   *Vase dating from the Meiji period, c. 1910. Height, 3½" (8.89 cm). Has a cobalt blue ground with gilt fans, each of which is filled with a differing diaper. Around the shoulder on two sides is a key fret pattern in gilt. There are two panels; one with a warrior and the other with seated bijin. The base is marked Satsuma yaki in gilt.*

170   *Toothpick holder dating from the Meiji period, c. 1905. Height, 1¾" (4.445 cm). The upper and lower borders are bands of nishikide diapers. The continuous motif is a riverbank with a mother and children walking through the grasses and flowers. Signed Kinkozan.*

171   Vases (pair) dating from the Meiji period, c. 1905. Height, 2½" (5.715 cm). Decorated in millefleur in colors and gilt on a gilt speckled ground. Two oval medallions are featured. Each depicts a family.

172   Saki pot dating from the Meiji period, c. 1900. Height, 3¾" (9.525 cm). The overall motif of alternating bands of nishikide diapers and the millefleur pattern is continuous and extends to the lid. The handle and spout are black with gilt flower heads. The form is hexagonal and there are panels on each side which depicts scenic motifs of a mother, father, and children on a terrace overlooking a lake and flower garden. Signed Hozan.

173 *Vase dating from Meiji period, c. 1910. Height, 3½" (8.89 cm). There are two heart-shaped medallions, one showing three seated bijin and an attendant on a veranda, the other showing three seated warriors and an attendant on a veranda. The uppermost band is annomite shell in gilt. The overall ground is black with flower heads in colors. The lowest band is a depiction of garden flowers in colors and gilt on a gilt speckled ground with a red band on the foot trim. Signed Seikozan.*

174 *Vase dating from the Meiji period, c. 1900. Height, 3½" (8.89 cm). The cobalt blue ground is decorated with gilt flower heads and scrolls and mons in the form of myoga (an herb of the ginger family) in gilt surrounded by gilt cloud forms. Featured are two panels, each of which has a finely enameled waterfowl among flowers and foliage on a gilt speckled ground.*

175   Saki pitcher dating from the Meiji period, c. 1910. Height, 5¼" (13.335 cm). The finial is of a lizard, and this is continued as the lizard forms the spout and handle. Finial, spout, the body entwined around the saki pitcher, and the handles are molded in relief. There are various medallions featuring vignettes of rakan and warriors.

176   Saki pot dating from the Meiji period, c. 1910. Height, 3½" (8.89 cm). The cover is decorated in millefleur polychrome on a gilt ground. This pattern is continued throughout and surrounds two heart-shaped reserves which feature a family on a veranda. This specimen stands on three legs and has a lower band of gilt diapers on a black ground. Signed Hozan.

177 (L to R) Teapot dating from the Meiji-Taisho period, c. 1915. The motif of rakan and dragon are set against scenic vignettes. The base has several markings including Choshuzan, Satsuma, Kuni. (See Fig. 149.) Teapot dating from the Showa period, c. 1926-1935. The motif is the same as the teapot to the left. Detail is a bit cruder and the colors less vibrant.

178 Partial tea set (cup and saucer with creamer) dating from the Showa period, c. 1930. The motif is the same as that in the preceding photograph. The interior of the cup is decorated with flower heads.

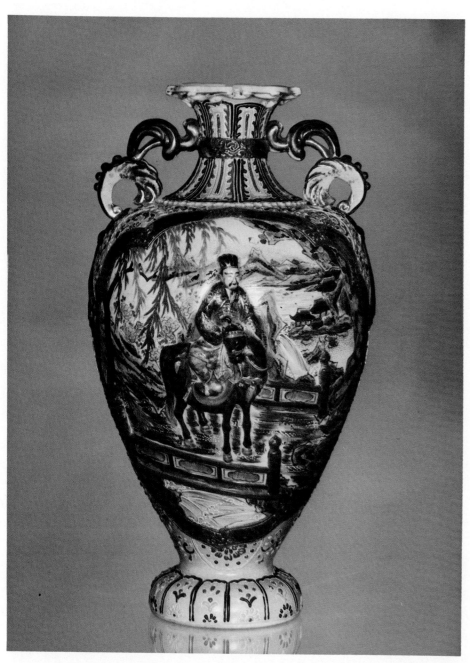

180   *Vase dating from the Taisho period, c. 1915. Height, 2" (5.08 cm). Covered with cobalt blue, the motif consists of bands of alternating and varied diapers and two panels filled with garden flowers. The only coloring used on the monochrome ground is gold. The silver overlay forms many of the flower petals.*

179   *Vase dating from the Taisho period, c. 1918. Height, 16½" (41.91 cm). Decorated with trailed enamels, the central motif is molded in relief and features a dignitary on horseback crossing a bridge. The dignitary, horse, and bridge are molded in relief and the scenic background and foreground are realistically enameled in colors. There are gilt accents on the details of the horse's trappings and within the garb of the dignitary.*

10 *The Mon and Other Marks*

The Japanese term "mon" may be translated to mean family crest, coat of arms, or emblem of heraldic bearing. The mon is found on many classes of wares in addition to Satsuma. This ornamental emblem was used as personal identification for Japanese families. In the 11th century, high ranking courtiers used specifically patterned textiles for formal costumes. The ruling family (Fujiwara) brought about the use of specific symbols as an identification for each family. The mon was placed on three areas of the costume: the left sleeve, the right sleeve, and on the upper back. By the end of the 12th century, the warrior class initiated the use of the mon on their flags, weapons, etc., and such was used as an identification during times of battle.

The courtiers and members of their household used the same mon. The warrior class allowed only members of the family to use the same emblem, with variations of the specific mon being used by their retainers.

By the Edo period, the mon was used by the merchant class as well. The mon became more flamboyant and stylized. From the Meiji period on, the mon was used by various classes as well as shops, companies, corporations, and cities much as our registered trademarks are used.

The mon of Shimazu family (gosu blue) is the only authentic Satsuma mon. It can be found used in combination with the Imperial mon, Tokugawa mon, as well as having been incorporated into motifs.

Marks

It is important to remember that it was not uncommon for Japanese marks or seals to be bartered, forged, or copied. The same markings were often used by several generations of the same family. Lesser known potters, producers, artists, or factories thought there was nothing wrong with using the mark or seal of a more famous potter, artist, or producer. Such is the case with the mon of the Shimazu family.

The mon of the Shimazu family (see Fig. 19A) has the form of a cross within a circle. Prior to the Meiji restoration, this marking almost always appeared in gosu (blue). It was used on Satsuma wares which the daimyo felt were meritorious.

(This should not be anyone's sole guide as to whether a particular object is indeed meritorious.) The daimyo allowed his seal to be used as an incentive in conjunction with annuities which were granted to his potters, thus encouraging his artisans to strive for a higher degree of excellence within their craft. This method of marking is significant in that it allows even the layman to make an immediate identification as to age. An object marked with the mon of the Shimazu clan in gosu (blue) would have been made prior to 1872. When one finds the cross and circle in a hue other than gosu, it indicates that such a piece was likely made no earlier than 1868.

The mon, in hues other than gosu (blue), appears on Satsuma and Satsuma style wares produced during the Taisho and Showa periods, as well as during the Meiji period.

From 1871, the daimyo were reduced to governors. Provinces (the previous domains of the daimyo) were revamped, and prefectures were established. Finally, the governors were forced to resign their positions and were replaced by government officials. Marks and mons, including that of the Shimazu family, appear on wares made after 1871, but they do not denote the official positions held by the daimyo prior to the Meiji restoration.

Often, interestd parties refer to the mon as the mark of the Prince of Satsuma. In actuality the title, ''Prince,'' was not used until 1885, and from 1871 on the former daimyo had nothing whatsoever to do with ceramic production. After the start of the Meiji period, ceramic production was the full responsibility of the individuals, companies, artists, and potters who ran private operations and businesses completely disassociated from any former fiefs. In 1885, the Emperor Meiji instituted five orders: Prince, Marquise, Count, Viscount, and Baron. Eleven of the former territorial chiefs (daimyo) were bestowed with the title of Prince. Therefore, the term ''Prince'' (or Imperial) in connection with Satsuma ceramics is totally inaccurate.

To further complicate the use of markings for purposes of authenticating age and value, is the misconception of country of origin markings. Collectors and interested parties will note that with regard to Satsuma and Satsuma-style wares produced from 1891 on there will seldom be a marking to indicate the country of origin. The McKinley Tariff Act of 1891 was instituted in order to provide consumers with the knowledge of what they were buying by knowing where such an item was produced. In the original McKinley Tariff Act it was specified that all articles of foreign manufacture would be plainly marked, stamped, branded, or labeled in legible English words so as to indicate the country of origin. From

1891 to March 21, 1921, the word Nippon was acceptable as proper marking for country of origin for goods manufactured in Japan and exported to the United States. Later, Treasury Decision #36989 used the words ''gummed label'' and ''rubber stamp'' for the first time. It was always assumed that the use of an affixed sticker on Japanese export wares was not initiated until this decision of 1917. However, the term ''labeled'' in the 1891 Act also indicated an affixed sticker. Therefore, we find that the use of labels has been acceptable as markings indicating country of origin since March 1, 1891. The following is a quote from the Tariff Act of October 3, 1913.

> Paragraph F/subsection 1: That all articles of foreign manufacture or production which are capable of being marked, stamped, branded or labeled, without injury, shall be marked, stamped, branded or labeled in legible English words, in a conspicuous place that shall not be covered or obscured by any subsequent attachments or arrangement, so as to indicate the country of origin. Said marking, stamping, branding or labeling shall be as nearly indelible and permanent as the nature of the article will permit.
>
> All packages containing imported articles shall be marked, stamped, branded or labeled so as to indicate legibly and plainly, in English words, the country of origin and the quantity of their contents, and until marked in accordance with the direction prescribed in this section, no articles or packages shall be delivered to the importer.

The second paragraph indicates that packages (meaning containers of imported items) were to be marked in the same manner as the items themselves.

It is reasonable to assume that from time to time there were methods employed by importers whereby merchandise was allowed to pass through U.S. Customs without close inspection. It may be assumed that on many occasions the labeling, branding, stamping, or markings of the container (with the contents left unmarked) was sufficient to pass through inspection by U.S. Customs. It is also probable that the importer would then remove the affixed label, and, similarly, the consumer did the same after making the purchase. (See Fig. 192A.)

This therefore would account for the lack of country of origin markings on Satsuma and Satsuma-style wares produced from 1891 on. This lack of marking indicating country of origin is not a clear and precise indication that the correct age of such an item would be prior to 1891.

It would appear that markings can help only in a limited way with regard to evaluation of age, authenticity, merit, and value, with the exception of the mon in gosu (blue).

For the layman, markings have even less meaning. However, there seems to be an overwhelming interest in marks on the part of interested parties as well as collectors. These interested parties show a preference to titling Satsuma by the name of the potter or artist whose signature, seal, or mark appears either on the base or within the motif. For this purpose, authentic renderings of marks have been reproduced for this book, and all the markings have been taken from actual specimens that have been authenticated by this writer-collector.

181   *Vase-bottle dating from the Showa period, c. 1926-1934. Height, 3¾" (9.525 cm). The ornamentation consists of various garden flowers in colors and gilt outlines. The lower band has a gilt scroll on a red brown ground. The upper band, shoulder, and neck have varying diapers executed in gilt on a black ground.*

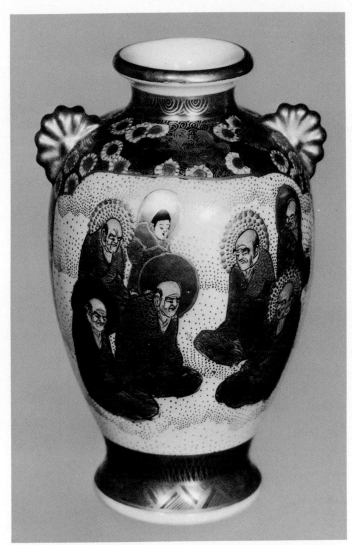

182   *Vase dating from the Meiji period, c. 1910. Height 3¾" (9.525 cm). The elongated neck is decorated with the millefleur pattern and mons in colors on a gilt ground. Surrounding the two heart-shaped reserves are various diapers in colors and gilt. One reserve features warriors; the other features courtesans.*

183   *Vase dating from the Taisho period, c. 1925. Height, 5" (12.7 cm). Two panels feature rakan against cloud formations of speckled gilt. The panels are framed by a ground covered with colors and gilt in the millefleur pattern. Upper and lower bands contain varied diapers in gilt on a black ground. The ears are half kiku. The base is marked with a gold cross and circle and markings which read Dai Nihon.*

186   *Vase dating from the Meiji period, c. 1915. Height, 3¾" (9.525 cm). This vase has a bulbous body and an elongated neck. Two identical, heart-shaped reserves, each depicting three children, are framed with flower heads enameled in colors and gilt. This ornamentation extends upward to the rim of the neck. Signed Shuzan.*

184   *Vase dating from the Taisho period, c. 1925. Height, 7½" (19.05 cm). Standing on a flared foot, the largest panel features a family dining on a veranda overlooking a lake scene. Other reserves are in various geometric contours and feature one thousand butterflies, one thousand flowers, etc. The ground surrounding the panel and reserves has arrays of various floral sprays including irises, plum blossoms, chrysanthemum heads, etc. The shoulder is enameled with nishikide diapers over which are enameled flower heads forming a rather busy network of pattern.*

185   *Vase dating from the Taisho period, c. 1920. Height, 8" (20.32 cm). The central theme is continuous rectangular panels, each depicting a different interpretation of rakan alternating with an interpretation of bijin and attendants. The overall ground is enameled in gilt and colors in various diapers. This specimen stands on a flared double foot trim, with a tapered waist flaring out to form a five-petaled formation. Markings include a gilt cross and circle, Dai Nihon, and Satsuma yaki.*

188   (L to R) Vase dating from the Showa period, c. 1935. Height, 5" (12.7 cm). This vase has a matt black ground with a gilt motif featuring a village with Mt. Fuji in the background. The reverse has a continuing motif with silver enamel added sparingly to the design. Vase dating from the Taisho period, c. 1925. Height, 7½" (19.05 cm). The same contour as the vase on the left, this piece has an overall motif of birds and wisteria enameled in colors and gilt.

187   Vase dating from the Taisho period, c. 1915. Height, 3½" (8.89 cm). Ovoid in form, vase has two panels, one depicting an adult and child at the lakeside, the other an array of flowers. The panels are framed with the millefleur pattern executed in colors and gilt on a gilt ground. The lower portion of the vase has a band of foliage and a band of diamond patterns in gilt on a black ground. Signed Shuzan.

189   Cup and saucer dating from the Showa period, either just prior to or following WW II. The pattern consists of butterflies in various sizes applied under and over the netting. The butterflies are finely enameled in colors and gilt. The bow and tassel add a pleasing effect.

190   (L to R) Top row: Button dating from the Meiji period, c. 1910. The outer border is cobalt blue with gilt dots. The motif shows two bijin and their attendant. Their kimonos are vividly enameled in colors and gilt. Button dating from the Showa period, c. 1938. The motif is bamboo with slight gilt outlining. Bottom row: Button dating from the Taisho period, c. 1922. The motif shows a bijin and child with parasol against a ground of speckled gilt with polychrome butterflies. Button dating from the Meiji period, c. 1900. The form is foliate and the motif of a lakeside shows waterfowl and foliage on a speckled gilt ground. Pin dating from the Meiji period, c. 1910. This pin has a brass backing. The motif of peony blossoms and chrysanthemums with foliage is finely enameled in blue, lavender, and pink with gilt outlining.

191   Vases (pair) dating from the Taisho period, c. 1925. Height, 6" (15.24 cm). This pair has a continuous motif of rakan and Kannon with other Buddhist disciples framed by cobalt blue panels. The blue panels have various diapers executed in gilt with gilt flower heads interspersed throughout.

192   *Vase dating from the Taisho-Showa period,
c. 1924-1927. Height, 5¾" (14.605 cm). This is an
important specimen in that the base has the original
sticker (label), and it confirms this author's research
in dating for the Kinkozan line of potters. The vase
features two panels. The one pictured shows women
and children molded in relief and enameled in gilt
with colors highlighting the overall concept. The
panel on the reverse features children and rakan molded in relief and enameled in gilt with colors. These
panels are framed in cobalt blue with gilt. The gilt,
somewhat worn from handling, is laid on in various
diapers, scrolls, and flower heads.*

192A   *Base of the vase shown in Fig. 192. The
label reads, S. Kinkozan with the style number and
place of origin, Kyoto, Japan. When turned around,
one can see the marking "Kinkozan tsukuru" (made
by Kinkozan) in red. (See section on markings and
country of origin.)*

193   *A complete set of buttons dating from the
Taisho-Showa period, c. 1923-1927. The buttons
have a motif of kiri mons in turquoise on a gilt-flecked
ground framed by a cobalt blue border with choji hana
bishi diapers in gilt. This set of buttons is in its
original box which has its original label still intact.
The label reads, "S. Kinkozan manufacturer of fine
porcelains, Kyoto Japan, Established 1645." Also
contained in this box was the card prepared by S.
Kinkozan which reads, "Gold Medal Paris
1900/Grand Prix Hanoi 1902/Medal of Honour
Osaka 1903/Kinkozan Pottery/Awata, Kyoto/
Japan/Established 1645. Tourists are respectfully invited to the pottery where a large stock in fine art
porcelain is always on exhibition. Visitors will un-
doubtedly be much interested in watching the process
of manufacture from the raw clay to the exquisitely
finished products."*

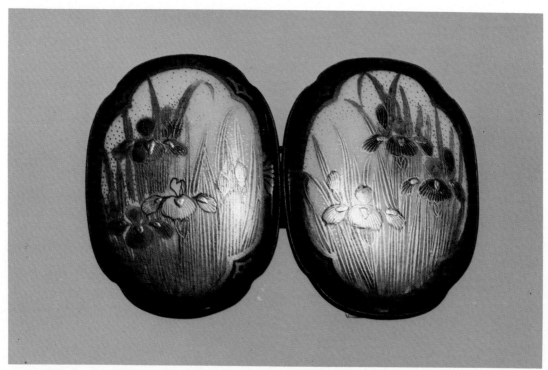

194   *Belt buckle dating from the Meiji period, c. 1905. Irises enameled in lavender and blue with green foliage and gilt outlining on a speckled gilt ground are framed in cobalt blue. The mounting is sterling silver (gin).*

195   *Cigarette box dating from the Showa period, just prior to WW II. Dimensions, 4¾″ × 4″ × 1¾″ (12.065 cm × 10.16 cm × 4.445 cm). The box is covered with the millefleur pattern in colors on a gilt ground. The base is marked Shofu.*

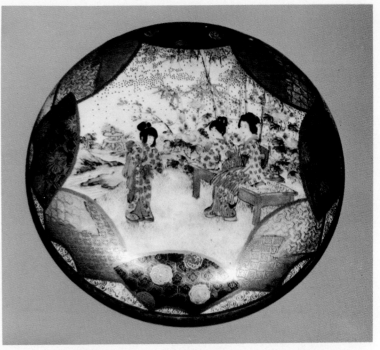

196   *Powder box dating from the Taisho period, c. 1923.
Diameter, 5½" (13.335 cm). The base is marked Satsuma and
Made in Japan (likely produced in Japan for Irice Products,
N.Y.C.). The ground is glazed, but there is no crackling what-
soever.*

197   *Powder box dating from the Meiji period, c. 1905. Diameter, 4¾"
(12.065 cm). The central motif of two children and a woman (mother and her
children) at the riverbank enjoying the flora and fauna is framed by fans, each of
which contains one or two diapers in gilt on a black or red ground. The base has
a gold cross and circle (mon) and a mark reading Hozan.*

198   *Powder box dating from the Taisho period, c. 1924. Diameter, 6" (15.24 cm). This box stands on three legs. The cover shows
bijin on a veranda with a panel depicting a peacock amid flowers and foliage. The interior shows a woman and child frolicking in tall
grasses. The exterior of the box has geometric reserves filled with various flowers including wisteria and chrysanthemums.*

199   *Kogo dating from the Meiji period, c.
1900. Height, 1¾", width, 2" (4.445 cm ×
5.08 cm). The lid of this kogo is decorated
with karako in colors on a gilt speckled ground.
The interior of the lid is enameled with butterflies in colors and gilt. The remainder of the
kogo is enameled in the millefleur pattern
which features chrysanthemums and peony
blossoms. The frame has a black ground with
white and gilt dots. Signed Meizan.*

200   *Plate dating from the Taisho period, c. 1920. Diameter, 12" (30.48 cm). The panel shows a
daimyo on horseback with his entourage of samurai and attendants who carry flags decorated with
blue, red, and black diapers. The frame is cobalt blue with gilt maple leaves and branches. The markings on the base read, "Dai Nihon Kyoto Shozan."*

11 Comparison Study
and Value Determination

The following is an excerpt from an article which was written by this collector and published in the Oriental Art Society of Chicago *Newsletter.* (See Bibliography.)

Past published books in which Satsuma wares are discussed indicate that during the Meiji period ''imitations'' of Satsuma wares were produced in areas such as Awata, Tokyo, Osaka, Yokohama, etc. It is the view of this writer-collector that it is perfectly acceptable to call the same wares, made in different locations, by the same name. Such is the case with English Staffordshire wares, as well as many other wares, and such a definition is applicable to Satsuma as well.

Other authors make reference to the Satsuma wares (so-called imitations) mass produced during the Meiji period as ''overladen,'' ''offensive,'' ''a scorn laden ware,'' ''overdecorated,'' ''terrible, ornate, and over detailed,'' which opinions have been foisted upon unknowing and unsuspecting Westerners. The emphasis seems to have been placed on an opinionated accounting, signifying that Meiji period Satsuma wares were mere copies of a more dignified and refined product, poorly executed and in bad taste, deserving no recognition whatsoever.

It is true that the elaborately (and I might add painstakingly) decorated Satsuma wares were not made in the Japanese tradition (especially those pieces which have human figures incorporated in the motifs); however, collectors are not as discriminating as these authors would lead one to believe. I find the viewpoints of these writers to be out of step with the times, considering that the last book of any significance was written over 25 years ago, and that one of the leading books was written during WW II. (I find this book shows a biased approach, which was perhaps influenced by world events of that particular time.) It is not difficult to understand why the faux pas exists. How can collectors and interested parties digest a new approach, if such an approach has not been publically stated. It is about time that the Satsuma export wares of the Meiji period are judged with the same considerations afforded wares produced during the Edo period.

It is the opinion of this writer that comparisons should not be made between pieces of different periods. Comparisons should be made only with pieces which are of like kind. That is: pieces of the same period; works of the same school; works which feature like techniques and methods in decoration and motif; works of the same artist or potter (including comparisons of earlier to later works produced by the same artist-potter), etc.

This collector does not discriminate and believes in a diversified collection. However, within a diversified collection, one can form special preferences for wares of a specific period, artist, and technique. Many collectors are extremely taken with early or middle period wares due to the softness and richness of enamel combinations and the total accuracy of potting and execution, all of which were accomplished without the advantage of modern methods and technology. Early and middle period wares provide superb objets d'art, the sum of which has never been recaptured. There are collectors and others who show preference for specific artists within the modern period, and there are those who have differing preferences.

Several factors are used as a guide in determining value and merit. Perhaps the most important criterion is age. Pieces of the early and middle periods are difficult to find because of their age and the fact that they were not produced in large quantities, as compared to modern period wares. Basically early and middle period wares were made for the sole use of the daimyo, shogunate, or Imperial court. Thus, not having been made for export, they are authentic "limited editions" in their own right.

One should not expect to find wares of the early and middle periods to be in perfect condition, although the majority of the early and middle period objects pictured in this volume are in perfect to near perfect condition. Condition does not play a major role with regard to merit and value when applied to early and middle period wares. Pieces held in high esteem by the Japanese which were in need of repair were mended with gold lacquer. The repair was not hidden. (Most Westerners prefer hidden repairs.) Such a repair can be found on a small area of the interior of the base rim of the koro in Fig. 16. This type of repair or any professional restoration does not diminish the value of an early or middle period piece, due to their limited availability.

Almost as important as age is availability. Pieces which are rare (for example: Satsuma decorated blanks, Edo period objects with a gosu [blue] mon, pieces of unusual size or contour), have higher values than pieces which are more abundant on today's market.

Another important consideration is quality of workmanship. One must take into account the merit of the decorator, potter, or producer. Hastily applied motifs, crude or haphazard application of enamels, or poor potting will detract from the overall merit of an object.

Style and method of decoration are important considerations when evaluating value and merit. One should always be on the watch for the unusual. For example: moriage motifs on modern and middle period wares or jeweled motifs of the middle period. The style of a particular artist, decorator, or potter will add greatly to the value and merit of an object, especially if the artist is well known and the piece bears an authentic marking.

Consideration must also be given to size and contour. One should look for pieces in which the contour is compatible with the motif. The subject matter and application of design should be balanced against the body (with the exception of pieces of the early period, as they show more assymmetry than later periods and were not produced for foreign export). With pieces of the modern period, one should look for that which is not ordinary. That is, unusual finials, handles, legs, and sizes (under 8″ and over 12″).

It is always the choice of the collector to weigh all the factors before making a final evaluation as to the worthiness of a particular piece. One must always remember the time and effort afforded to the creation of an object. One should always take the time to assess the relationship of a particular piece against its price. The choice is the buyer's alone.

201   Kogo dating from the Meiji period, c. 1905. Diameter, 4" (10.16 cm). Ogi (scalloped) shape, the photograph shows both the cover and the interior of the base. The interior of the cover is decorated in the same manner as the interior of the base. The theme on the cover shows samurai and bijin on a veranda overlooking a garden of irises. This kogo is enameled in colors and gilt.

202   Kogo dating from the Meiji period, c. 1910. Diameter, 3¾" (9.525 cm). Both the interior of the lid and the base are enameled; the base with a bird, butterfly, tree stump, and grasses; the interior of the lid with wisteria, peony blossoms, and mums with birds in flight. The cover shows courtesans having a celebration at the riverbank. Ogi shape.

203   *Kogo dating from the Meiji period, c. 1910. Diameter, 2¾" (6.985 cm). The interior is an enameled river scene with Mt. Fuji in the background. The scenic exterior features figures of men, women, and children entering and leaving a temple. The kogo is hexagonal and signed Kinkozan.*

204   *Kogo dating from the Meiji period, c. 1900. Height 1¼", width, 1½" (3.175 cm × 3.81 cm). The ground is cobalt blue with a pattern of gilt annomite shell. The panel shows a woman and two children reading. The motif is set on a gilt-speckled ground and executed in colors and gilt. The interior of the lid and base are decorated with flowers in colors and gilt.*

205   *Kogo dating from the Meiji period, c. 1895-1910. Diameter, 3" (7.62 cm). Glazed overall in cobalt blue with gilt chrysanthemum heads, the motif shows samurai entertaining bijin. The motif is executed in colors and gilt with extensive gilt diapers on the kimonos. The interior shows three bijin holding hagoita (a battledore used in playing Hanatsuki, a paddle game). The base has markings which read, ''Dai Nihon Satsuma yaki.''*

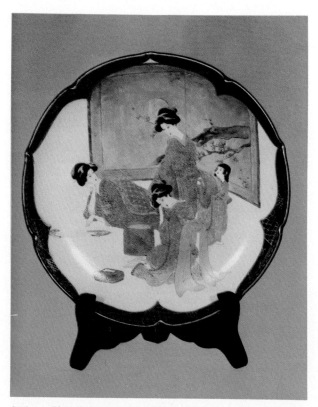

206   Plate dating from the Taisho period, c. 1925. Diameter,
7" (17.78 cm). Ogi (foliate-scalloped) contour and cobalt blue rim
with gilt diapers framing an ogi-shaped panel featuring three bijin
and attendant-child in leisurely poses. One bijin is reading a letter, and the other is adjusting her hairdo. A two-panel screen in
the background gives a three-dimensional illusion. The markings
read, "Dai Nihon Satsuma yaki Buzan."

207   Box dating from the Meiji period, c. 1900-1910. Diameter, 5¼" (13.335 cm). The covered box has a flat
knob and is decorated with various flowers and foliage. Signed Kinkozan.

208   (L to R) Top row: Vase dating from the Taisho period, c. 1915. Height, 8½" (21.59 cm). Poorly enameled, with enamels daubed on, the neck is ornamented with knife cuts. Figure dating from the Meiji period, c. 1900. Height, 10½" (26.67 cm). The figure of Kannon is termed Satsuma style (it is porcelain) and was likely made at Kutani-Ishikawa prefecture. Vase dating from the Meiji period, c. 1895. Height, 8½" (21.59 cm). Vase dating from the Taisho-Meiji period, 1925-1930. Height, 7" (17.78 cm). Second row: Pair of vases dating from the Meiji period, c. 1900. Height, 7" (17.78 cm). Glazed in cobalt blue with gilt flower heads, vases have two panels featuring bijin in a scenic expression with cherry blossoms. Bowl dating from the Taisho-Showa period, c. 1925-1935. Diameter, 7½" (19.05 cm). The motif is Kannon with a rakan on either side. Vase dating from the Taisho period, c. 1915. Height, 7½" (19.05 cm). The motif consist of white mums with birds and flowers on a ground which shades from yellow to blue. Third row: Vase dating from the Taisho period, c. 1920. Height, 9½" (24.13 cm). Enamels are daubed on in a crude manner. Vase dating from the Taisho period, c. 1915. Height, 12½" (31.75 cm). Vase dating from the Taisho period, c. 1915. Height, 12½" (31.75 cm). The enamels are daubed on in a crude manner, however. Vase dating from the Taisho period, c. 1925. Height, 7½" (19.05 cm).

209   *(L to R) Top row: Vase dating from the Taisho period, c. 1915. Height, 12" (30.48 cm). Dark iron red ground with motif of irises and foliage with bold gilt outlining. Vase dating from the Meiji period, c. 1910. Height, 12½" (31.75 cm). Shaded deep green ground with Shi Shi and ringed ears, the bold gilt motif is of a phoenix. Vase dating from the Meiji period, c. 1905. Height, 12" (30.48 cm). The neck has reticulated motifs, and the rim was ornamented with knife cutouts. The motif was executed in trailed enamels. Bottom row: Vase dating from the Meiji period, c. 1900. Height, 16½" (41.91 cm). Has Kirin handles and a fluted rim with neck extension featuring reticulated ornamentation. The base is shaded from the light to dark pink with a blue body containing a medallion of chrysanthemum heads, flower heads, and scrolls. Vase dating from the Meiji period, c. 1905. Height, 15" (38.1 cm). Phoenix handles with a scalloped, overhanging rim decorate vase with alternating polychrome and gilt diapers. The motif of irises and foliage lies against an iron red ground. The flared foot has a band of nishikide diapers. Vase dating from the Meiji period, c. 1900. Height, 16" (40.64 cm). Blue seahorse handles on neck and foot. The body is pink with a floral reserve and mon. When turned sideways the contour is that of a fish (perhaps a kissing gourami).*

210   *(L to R) Top row: Vases (pair) dating from the Meiji period, c. 1910. Height, 12" (30.48 cm). The motif features geisha and attendants. The motif has various diapers throughout. Vase dating from the Taisho period, c. 1915. Height, 12" (30.48 cm). The motif features a samurai and attendant with overall nishikide diapers. Bottom row: Vases (pair) dating from the Meiji period, c. 1909. Height, 12" (30.48 cm). Ringless elephant-head handles with motifs of two samurai in battle. Nishikide diapers throughout. Vase dating from the Meiji period, c. 1910. Height, 18" (45.72 cm). The motif shows samurai. Neck is ornamented with knife cuts, and the handles have mock rings and nishikide diapers throughout.*

211 (L to R) Top row: Vase dating from the Taisho period, c. 1920. Height, 11½" (29.21 cm). The motif of leaves is boldly outlined. Coloring consists of browns and shades of green and turquoise. Vases (pair) dating from the Taisho period, c. 1915. Height, 12" (30.48 cm). Decorated with trailed enamels in colors and gilt, with two panels featuring samurai in a scene framed by trailed polychrome motifs on a matt brown ground. Bottom row: Vases (pair) dating from the Taisho period, c. 1915. Height, 16½" (40.64 cm). The front has a panel featuring samurai; reverse has a panel of flowers and foliage. The ground is turquoise blue with green and white flower heads throughout. The motifs were executed with trailed enamels in colors and gilt. Vase dating from the Meiji period, c. 1890. Height, 12" (30.48 cm). The netting motif in gilt increases in size around the central portion of the body and diminishes as it reaches the neck and foot trim. Delicately enameled in colors and gilt are pansies and foliage which appear lifelike.

212   (L to R) Top row: Vase dating from the Taisho period, c. 1915. Height, 12½″ (31.75 cm). Vase dating from the Showa period, c. 1930. Height, 8″ (20.32 cm). Vase dating from the Taisho period, c. 1920. Height, 12½″ (31.75 cm). Bottom row: Vase dating from the Taisho period, c. 1925. Height, 12¼″ (31.115 cm). Vase dating from the Taisho period, c. 1925. Height, 15½″ (39.37 cm). Vase dating from the Taisho period, c. 1925. Height, 12½″ (31.75 cm). All the vases in this photograph are quite common on today's market. They feature a motif of Kannon, Rakan, and, on occasion, a dragon is introduced as well. Generally there is somewhat of a scenic motif in the background. These vases can be found in both faience and porcelain. Prices for such specimens have not increased in the last few years due to the high availability. The last vase on the bottom row features a bijin and child and is more difficult to find.

Figs. 213 to 231 feature Satsuma blanks decorated in the United States.

213   Dish dating from the Taisho period, Christmas 1915. Diameter, 6" (15.24 cm). The motif is Art Nouveau in style and was executed in pink, baby blue, green, and gilt.

214   Bowl dating from the Taisho period, c. 1915. Diameter, 7¼" (18.415 cm). The bowl is hexagonal in form. The rim is decorated with a basket pattern in light and dark orange (Kaga-Kutani style). The motif of flowers and scrolls is enameled in orange, white, and mustard. There is a small flower in the center of the interior. The bowl is signed Timlin.

216   Kogo (box) dating from the Taisho period, c. 1925. Diameter, 2½" (6.35 cm). A most unusual Art Deco scenic design, with the base signed "Annie Cleveland." (West Coast school.)

215   Dish dating from the Meiji period, January 1911. Diameter, 6½" (16.51 cm). The motif is executed in shades of lavender, pink, blue, with green and gilt. The base is signed "Mearle Beatrice Hager January 1911."

217   Kogo (box) dating from the Taisho period, c. 1925. Diameter, 4½" (11.43 cm). This box is decorated with a flowing, Art Nouveau motif in the form of a peacock in various shades of blue accented with orange red and gilt. This is attributed to Annie Cleveland (the base signed "A.C.").

218   Bowl dating from the Taisho period, c. 1925. Diameter, 6" (15.24 cm). The interior is enameled with a flat blue green reminiscent of certain kinds of Chinese Export porcelains. The center reserve on the interior is an unusual combination of olive green and turquoise. The jewel-like gilt enamel and the progression of the motif lend a Tiffany effect to the overall concept. Signed "A. Cleveland."

219   Box dating from the Meiji period, c. 1930. Diameter, 4½" (11.43 cm). Meticulously decorated in floral motifs and attributed to Annie Cleveland.

220   Saki pot dating from the Meiji period, c. 1926-1933. This miniature is attributed to Gertrude Menken Houston, an East Coast artist. The motif is Art Deco. The interiors of the spout, lid, and rim are covered in gilt. This miniature stands on three squat legs.

12 Satsuma Style

Satsuma style wares are porcelain wares which have been mass produced since the turn of the century (c. 1900). Such wares are embellished with raised polychrome enamels and gilt, and generally they have an abundance of jeweling. Many of the Satsuma style wares produced during the 1920s have a deep chocolate, matt ground. Similar wares produced during the 1930s have a lighter ground which is more of a red brown hue. (These wares are still being manufactured in various places in Japan for Western export.)

Hints for the Layman

When evaluating age, color is an excellent guide. White or yellow outlining, especially on wares with trailed enamels (see Fig. 211), dates from c. 1915. Decorative pieces having dark grounds with motifs outlined in gold generally date from the turn of the century. Gosu (blue) dates prior to 1872 and oxidized cobalt blue dates from 1872 on.

There are notable differences between the wares produced during the Edo and Meiji periods and similar wares produced during the Taisho and Showa periods. On many of the later wares, the crackle is rather large, with the lines tending to be rather long, irregular, and greatly exaggerated or defined. On many of the later wares the dark blue and green grounds are somber, and the lighter hues are too vivid and intense.

Rim glazing is another aid in evaluating age. Prior to 1900, the rims of covers were generally left unglazed. During the Edo period, the entire underside of lids and covers were left unglazed, generally.

Satsuma wares were crafted by hand. One artist may have developed an object solely, or several artisans may have worked jointly on an individual object or a pair. An article may have been shaped by hand or by means of a potter's wheel. Enamels and designs were applied for the most part without the use of stencils. This kind of craftsmanship causes irregularities in size, contour, glazing, enameling, and design. Such irregularities are not imperfections. They simply add to the overall value and beauty of Satsuma.

221   Jar dating from the Taisho period, c. 1925. Height, 8"
(20.32 cm). The body is completely covered with jewel-like gilt
enamel. It has three curled legs, fish handles and finial. The flower
motif in colors lies upon a black ground with a small band of flowers
connecting the front motif to that on the back. Signed "Menton."

222   Nut set dating from the Taisho period, c. 1915. The set consists of
one large bowl and eight small bowls, with the largest bowl being square in
form and the smaller bowls being round. The foot trim on each piece is
enameled in blue. The interior of each piece has a medallion filled with
flower heads and foliage. Only the largest bowl has this motif carried over
to the exterior in the form of scallops.

223   Sugar and creamer dating from the Meiji period, c. 1910. Unsigned and from the East Coast school, this sugar and
creamer stand on circular bases with an overhang of scallops. The motif in the form of a band contains flowers and foliage against
a gilt-speckled ground. The design is executed in shades of pale blue and yellow. Handles, spout, finial, and rims are trimmed in
gilt. The overall effect simulates lampshades (Tiffany style).

225   *Koro (incense burner) dating from the Showa period, c. 1928. Undecorated but obviously meant for the hands of an amateur or hobbyist. The base is impressed JAPAN.*

224   *Vase dating from the Taisho period, c. 1915. Height, 5" (12.7 cm). This cylindrical vase stands on three ruyi-shaped gilt feet. The motif has an array of flowers executed in Art Nouveau style in shades of pink, lavender, and blue on a speckled gilt ground.*

226   *Bowl dating from the Taisho period, c. 1925. Diameter, 8¼" (20.955 cm). This hexagonal-shaped bowl is decorated with a combination of blue and gilt accented by alternating reserves of flowers and birds. The interior has a large center floral reserve. The bowl is signed "Herrick."*

227   Bowl dating from the Showa period, c. 1940. The motif is quite simple and consists of
grapes and foliage with gilt bands.

229   Kogo (box) dating from the Taisho
period, c. 1924. Diameter, 3½˝ (8.89 cm).
The motif in pale shades of blue and purple
with gilt is of a peacock with the motif showing
flowing lines. Signed S. Anderson.

228   Bowl dating from the Taisho period, c. 1924. Diameter, 5˝ (12.70 cm). Hexagonal in form, the motif consists of a band of
flower heads with circular motifs in colors and gilt. The base is impressed JAPAN.

230   Koro (incense burner) dating from the Taisho period, c. 1925.
The base is signed C.H. Kerry. The motif is transitional and shows the
Art Nouveau influence as well as the Art Deco influence.

231   Koro (incense burner) dating from the Taisho period, c. 1923.
Diameter, 4½″ (11.43 cm). The cover is gilt and the motif consists of
bands of flower heads and panels of floral sprays. The base is marked with
the artist's initials, M.H.C., and an impressed mark, JAPAN.

Figs. 232 through 235 show Satsuma style wares (porcelain-bodied objects).

232   (L to R) Top row: Satsuma style cup
and saucer dating from the Meiji period, c.
1900. The motif consists of reserves showing
scenic views and children. Demitasse cup and
saucer dating from the Showa period, c. 1935.
Eggshell porcelain with motif of flowers. Bottom row: Satsuma style dishes dating from the
Meiji period, c. 1910. The motif consists of
scenic medallions and diapers. Satsuma style
syrup pitcher dating from the Meiji period, c.
1910. Motif is the same as the accompanying
dishes.

233   (L to R) Top row: Koro dating from the Taisho period, c. 1925. Height, 10" (25.4 cm). This piece has three masked feet, Shi Shi handles and a Shi Shi and tama finial. Vase dating from the Showa period, c. 1930. Height, 7" (17.78 cm). Shi Shi handles. Second row: Teapot, elephant figural dating from the Showa period, c. 1935. Teapot, elephant figural dating from the Showa period, c. 1930. The teapot on the left has a pagoda finial, and the teapot on the right has a mahout finial. Third row: Lamp base dating from the Showa period, c. 1930. Height, 7" (17.78 cm). Kannon upon an elephant. Teapot, elephant figural dating from the Taisho period, c. 1925. Lamp base dating from the Taisho period, c. 1925. Height, 6" (15.24 cm). Elephant with pagoda finial.

234　　(L to R) Top row: Tea set dating from the Showa period, c. 1935. Dragon finials and spouts with luster interiors.
Second row: Tea set dating from the Taisho period, c. 1925. Dragon finials, spouts, handles, with molded dragons around the
body of each serving piece. Third row: Tea set dating from the Showa period, c. 1930. Dragon finials and dragon spout on the
teapot only. Interiors with pearlized luster finish.

235   (L to R) Top row: Tea set dating from the Showa period, just prior to WW II. (These sets were also produced after the second World War and can be found in orange and green as well as blue. Such sets may also have
lithophane cups.) Second row: Saki bottle dating from the Showa period, c. 1935. Demitasse set dating from the
Showa period, c. 1935. In all likelihood, the saki cups had lithophane interiors. The demitasse set was also made as
coffee sets and tea sets. The motif is of a dragon in gold and red surrounded by red flames. Third row: Juice set consisting of six tumblers with pearlized luster interiors and an elephant figural juice pot with mahout finial dating from
the Taisho period, c. 1930. Third row: Vase dating from the Taisho period, c. 1925. Height, 6½″ (16.51 cm).
The dragon is molded in relief, and his head is in protrusion. Cookie jar dating from the Taisho period, c. 1920. Shi
Shi handles and finial. Planter in the form of a puppy dating from the Showa period, c. 1935. Height, 5″ (12.7 cm).

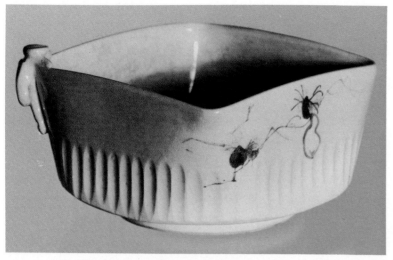

236   A tea bowl (cha wan) dating from the Edo period, late 17th-early 18th century. Height, 2½" (6.63 cm). Shiro Satsuma with sparse, pencillike sketches on the interior and exterior. The motifs were executed in under the glaze iron oxide and under the glaze blue. The interior motif is that of two twigs and leaves. On the exterior the motif resembles spiders. There are long, rice grain type repetitive motifs all around the body. This dish has a ringed foot and at one corner there is a figure peering over the rim.

237   A brazier (furo) dating from the Edo period, c. 1860-1870. Height, 9½" (25.18 cm). (Lid is a replacement.) The motifs of irises and leaves are extraordinarily bold. The ears form Shi Shi heads, and there are gilt highlights overall.

238   A double gourd bottle dating from the Meiji period, c. 1900. Height, 16" (42.40 cm). The brown body is covered with deep brown and brown black globules of glaze. This is a later form (facsimile) of earlier "Jakatstu" glazing. Pieces of this type and age are attributed to the productions of the Ryumonji kilns.

239   A large bottle dating from the 19th century. Satsuma in monochrome is not common. This particular specimen is 21" tall (55.65 cm). It has a beautiful yellow glaze which is finely crackled and slightly iridescent.

240   A tea caddy with a simple motif of waves and birds. This specimen dates from the Edo period, c. 1840. Height, 4" (10.60 cm). The pewter cap is decorated with dragons. The base has a blue mon.

241   Koro (incense burner) dating from the Edo period, c. 1860. Height, 5" (13.25 cm). Lid is surmounted by a Shi Shi. Overall motif is that of paulownia blossoms, leaves, scrolling vines, with professional restoration to cover.

242   A Satsuma style vase dating from the Meiji period, c. 1868-1872. Height, 10" (26.50 cm). This vase is one of the earliest specimens of "Satsuma styling" ever examined by this collector-researcher.

243   Teapot dating from the Meiji period, c. 1900. Height, 5½" (14.58 cm). For description see Fig. 238.

244   *Three-piece miniature mantle set consisting of matching bottle-form vases and incense burner, dating from the Taisho period, c. 1912-1925. Height of vases, 3¾" (9.94 cm); incense burner, 4¾" (12.59 cm). The overall motif on all three pieces is that of warriors on horseback engaged in battle with drawn swords. The vases are entwined with dragons. The koro has three masked feet, masked and ringed ears, and a Shi Shi finial. The motif was intricately executed in polychrome and gilt.*

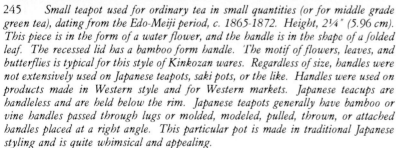

245   *Small teapot used for ordinary tea in small quantities (or for middle grade green tea), dating from the Edo-Meiji period, c. 1865-1872. Height, 2¼" (5.96 cm). This piece is in the form of a water flower, and the handle is in the shape of a folded leaf. The recessed lid has a bamboo form handle. The motif of flowers, leaves, and butterflies is typical for this style of Kinkozan wares. Regardless of size, handles were not extensively used on Japanese teapots, saki pots, or the like. Handles were used on products made in Western style and for Western markets. Japanese teacups are handleless and are held below the rim. Japanese teapots generally have bamboo or vine handles passed through lugs or molded, modeled, pulled, thrown, or attached handles placed at a right angle. This particular pot is made in traditional Japanese styling and is quite whimsical and appealing.*

246   *Vase, modified Mei P'ing form, dating from the Taisho period, c. 1915. Height, 7½" (19.88 cm). This particular specimen is attributed to a Wakayama kiln. It has a yellowy cream glaze with rather large crackles. Some specimens of this type shade from green to yellowy cream. The motif consists of stenciled mons and flying phoenixes executed in black, red, and gilt. The contour is pleasing and requires very little embellishment.*

140

Appendix
The Zodiacal Cycle and Year Periods (Nengo)

Characters		Name of period	Commenced A.D.	Characters		Name of period	Commenced A.D.
永	應	O-ei	1394	明	文	Bunmei	1469
長	正	Shocho	1428	享	長	Choko	1487
享	永	Eikio	1429	德	延	Entoku	1489
吉	嘉	Kakitsu	1441	應	明	Meio	1492
安	文	Bun-an	1444	亀	文	Bunki	1501
德	宝	Hotoku	1449	正	永	Eisho	1504
德	享	Kotoku	1452	永	大	Daiei	1521
正	康	Kosho	1455	禄	享	Koroku	1528
禄	長	Choroku	1457	文	天	Tembun	1532
正	寛	Kwansho	1460	治	弘	Koji	1555
正	文	Bunsho	1466	禄	永	Eirko	1558
仁	應	Onin	1467	亀	元	Genki	1570

Characters	Name of period	Commenced A.D.	Characters	Name of period	Commenced A.D.
天正	Tensho	1573	天和	Tenna	1681
文禄	Bunroku	1592	貞享	Jokio	1684
慶長	Keicho	1596	元禄	Genroku	1688
元和	Genna	1615	宝永	Hoei	1704
寬永	Kwanei	1624	正德	Shotoku	1711
正保	Shoho	1644	享保	Kioho	1716
慶安	Keian	1648	元文	Gembun	1736
承應	Jo-o	1652	寬保	Kwanpo	1741
明曆	Meireki	1655	延享	Enkio	1744
萬治	Manji	1658	寬延	Kwanen	1748
寬文	Kwambun	1661	宝曆	Horeki	1751
延宝	Empo	1673	明和	Meiwa	1764

Characters	Name of period	Commenced A.D.	Characters	Name of period	Commenced A.D.
永安	Anei	1772	政安	Ansei	1854
明天	Temmei	1781	延萬	Manen	1860
政寬	Kwansei	1789	久文	Bunkiu	1861
和享	Kiowa	1801	治元	Genji	1864
化文	Bunkwa	1804	應慶	Keio	1865
政文	Bunsei	1818	治明	Meiji	1868
保天	Tempo	1830	大正	Taisho	1912
化弘	Kokwa	1844	昭和	Showa	1926 to the present
永嘉	Kaei	1848			

Marks Section

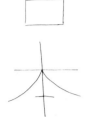

Nihon/Nippon (Japan in the Japanese language)

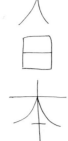

Dai Nihon/Dai Nippon (Great Japan)

Tokyo

Kyoto

Satsuma

Sei (made/manufactured/ produced)

Tsukuru (manufactured/created/produced)

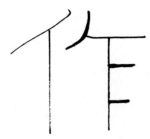

Saku (made — see Jizan)

Ga (painted)

These marks can appear singly or as part of an overall mark.

Hitsu (drawn)

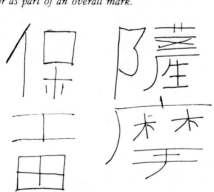

Satsuma Hododa

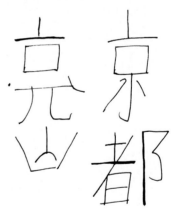

Kyoto Ryozan

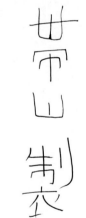

Taizan tsukuru

The mon of the Shimazu family

The Tokugawa mon (maru mitsu aoi) composed of three leaves of the asarum plant (wild ginger plant)

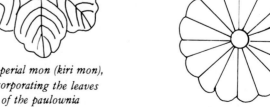

Imperial mon (kiri mon), incorporating the leaves of the paulownia

Imperial mon (kiku mon), chrysanthemoid form containing exactly sixteen petals

Satsuma

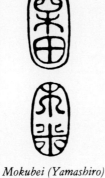

Satsuma

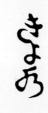

Mokubei (Yamashiro)

Awata (Kyoto School)

Kiyomizu (Kyoto School)

Bizan (Kyoto School)

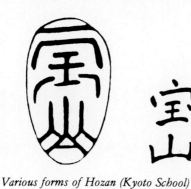

Various forms of Hozan (Kyoto School)

Rozan (Kyoto School)

Kinunken (Kyoto School)

Kozan
(Kiyomizu-Kyoto School)

Jizan (Kyoto School)

Seikozan (Kyoto School)

Various forms of Taizan (Awata-Kyoto School)

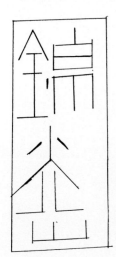

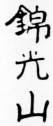

Various forms of Kinkozan (Awata-Kyoto School)

Two forms of Tanzan
(Awata-Kyoto School)

145

Various forms used by Shozan (Kyoto School)

Two forms used by Tozan (Gojozaka-Kyoto School)

      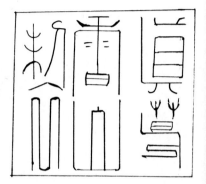

Various marks used by Miyagawa Kozan (Ota, Yokohama-Tokyo School)

Rozan (Tokyo School)

Eizan (Tokyo School)

Makuzu Kiln (Ota, Yokohama)

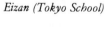

 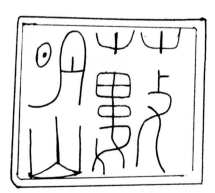  

Various marks used by Yabu Meizan (Osaka)

Keida (Masataro (Satsuma-Kagoshim

146

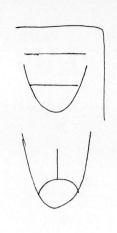

Shizan (Kyoto School)

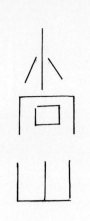

Jozan (Kyoto School)

Shuzan (Kyoto School)

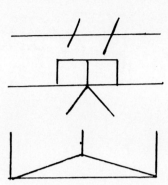

Eizan (Kyoto School)

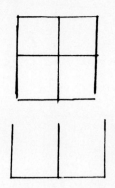

Denzan (Kyoto School)

Genzan (Satsuma-Kagoshima)

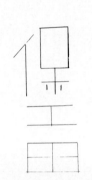

Hododa (Tokyo School)

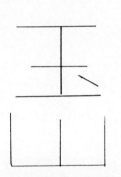

Gyokuzan (Chin Ju Kan)
(Satsuma-Kagoshima)

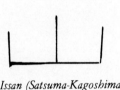

Issan (Satsuma-Kagoshima)

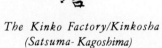

Nakajima (Satsuma-Kagoshima)

The Kinko Factory/Kinkosha
(Satsuma- Kagoshima)

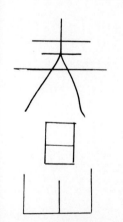

Shunzan
(Satsuma-Kagoshima)

Matsudaira
(Satsuma-Kagoshima)

Fuwa Sodo
(Satsuma-Kagoshima)

Two marks of the Iwakura kiln
(just north of Kyoto)

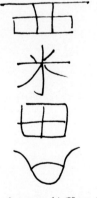

Awataguchi (Kyoto)

Ranzan
(Satsuma-Kagoshima)

Two forms of Seishi. Sometimes found in combination with an inscription that translates "Abundant Japanese Pottery Garden" (Tokyo School-Shiba District)

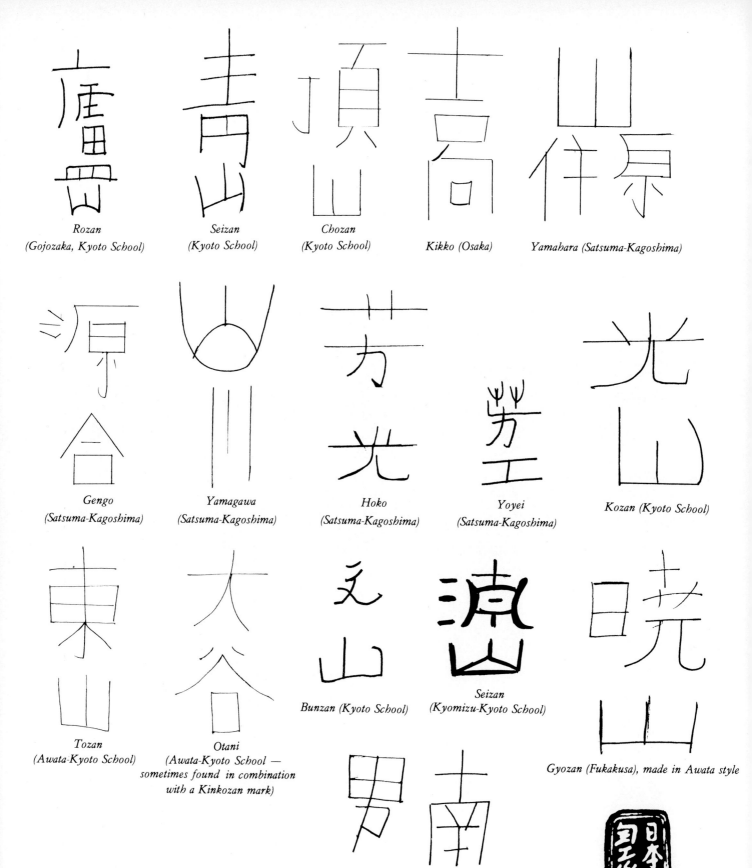

Rozan
(Gojozaka, Kyoto School)

Seizan
(Kyoto School)

Chozan
(Kyoto School)

Kikko (Osaka)

Yamahara (Satsuma-Kagoshima)

Gengo
(Satsuma-Kagoshima)

Yamagawa
(Satsuma-Kagoshima)

Hoko
(Satsuma-Kagoshima)

Yoyei
(Satsuma-Kagoshima)

Kozan (Kyoto School)

Tozan
(Awata-Kyoto School)

Otani
(Awata-Kyoto School —
sometimes found in combination
with a Kinkozan mark)

Bunzan (Kyoto School)

Seizan
(Kyomizu-Kyoto School)

Gyozan (Fukakusa), made in Awata style

Otokoyama (used from 1870 on
and produced in Awata style)

Nippon Tokyo Toko rakuga
(Tokyo School)

Marks found on Satsuma style wares.

M in Wreath

Plum Blossom

Pawlonia Blossom

Royal Satsuma Nippon

Gold Castle

Double T Diamond, Japan

O.G. Japan

Advertisements taken from the Japan Chronicle
1933-1934

149

Advertisements taken from the official catalog
issued by the Kyoto Commercial Museum, 1910.

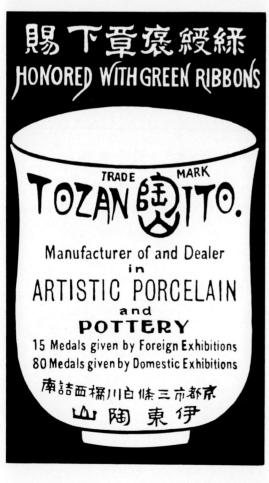

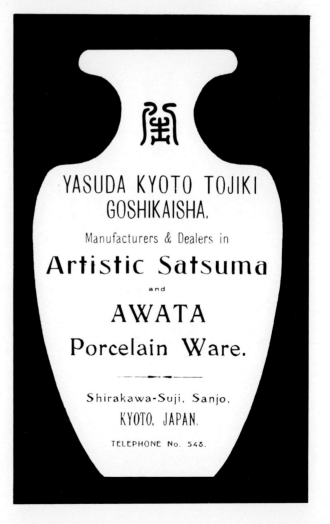

Motifs

Jardiniere base with elaborate diapers. (See Fig. 93.)

Close-up of nishikide diapers. (L to R) Choji hana bishi (cloves in a flower shaped diamond pattern); shokuko (a name for a Chinese textile); and cumo (clouds). The diaper at the bottom is termed shippo bishi (cloisonne diamond pattern).

Shippo bishi (cloisonne in a diamond pattern)

Shippo (seven precious things, cloisonne)

Mie dasuki (tasuki) (triple design of crossed swords)

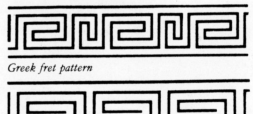

Greek fret pattern

Disconnected oblong fret pattern

Seikainami (blue sea waves) or Seigaiha (stylized waves)

Kumo (clouds)

Kumo (clouds)

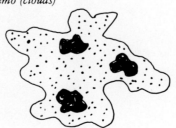

Saya gata (a fret pattern also termed Mani tsunagi/ Buddhist cross)

151

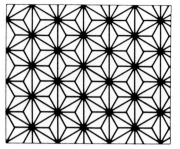

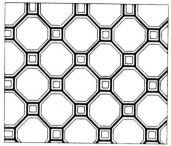

Asa no ha (a leaf of hemp)   *Tortoiseshell grids (kame)*   *Rai (lightning)*

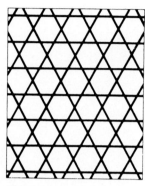

Floral lozenges

Uroko gata (fish scales)   *Shippo tsunagi (joined circles)*   *Komon (fine, small, repetitive patterns)*   *Kogome (woven basket pattern or basket pattern)*   *Yotsu bishi (quadruple lozenges or Nanbu)*

Higaki (cedar bark shingles or braided fence)   *Peony scroll*   *Karakusa (arabesque)*   *Gentian and foliage medallion*   *Chrysanthemum medallion*

Wave medallion   *Tomoe (comma mon)*   *Crane medallion*   *Genji-ko*   *Wisteria medallion*   *Aisu (swastika)*

A price list reproduced from a Vantine catalog which dates c. 1885.

Jardinieres.

Adapted for Palms, Bay-trees, Hydrangeas and fancy plants.

In effective designs and colorings, suitable for house, porch or lawn use. The interesting decorations of China are successfully used in this line.

Tokenabi Ware.

Red terra cotta, with raised dragon and cloud designs.

6 in. diameter, $ .25 each.
7 " " .35 "
8¾ " " .50 "
9¼ " " .75 "
10½ " " 1.00 "
13 " " 2.00 "

Owari Blue and White.

Hand-painted designs of flowers, vines and birds.

6 in. diameter, $ .75 each.
7 " " 1.25 "
8 " " 1.50 "
9½ " " 2.00 "
11 " " 3.00 "
13 " " 6.00 "

Umbrella Jars.

Far superior to the conventionel metal jardiniere—rich in colorings, unique in shapes. Round, cylindrical and fancy shapes. Sizes, 24 inches high, 9 inches in diameter.

Made in all wares and decorated with patterns suitable for halls and verandas.

Blue and white, floral and figured, with border, $1.50 each.

Chinese Blue and White, $10.00.

Imari red and blue, floral all over design, $1.75 each.

Tokenabi red terra cotta ware, repousse, dragon and cloud design, $1.50 plain. $1.75 gold design.

Sedji green glaze, with raised flower designs, painted in shades of blue, $4.50 each.

Satsuma, earthen body, painted in gold and colors of figures and temples, $3.50 each.

Taizan or solid color earthen jars in floral, vine and spray designs, $4.50 to 8.00.

Tokio, Kaga and fancy Satsuma and Sedji ware, appropriately painted in rich designs and colorings. Over 25 styles. $18.00 to 25.00.

Satsuma and Taizan, heavy gold figure and color paintings, assorted in design.

5½ in. diam. ass't colors, $ .50 each.
6 " " " " .75 "
9 " " " " 1.25 "
10 " " " " 2.00 "
12 " " " " 6.00 "

Chinese Water Kongs, earth brown body, decoration of heavy raised work; just the thing for lawns.

30 in. diam. $35.00 each.
23½ " " 25.00 "

Chinese Blue and white, dragon and floral designs.

Chinese five color painting, dragon and flowers.

Large Floor Vases.

We have abundant evidence of the Oriental's skill and cleverness in his vase and Koro productions; the treatments are uniformly beautiful and original

Blue and White Ware. Decorations of birds, flowers, dragons, landscape, etc., 3 to 6 feet high, $22.50, 60.00, 100.00, 175.00.

Imari Ware. Decorations of red, blue and gold in medallion and figure decoration; 2 to 4 feet high. $25.00, 35.00, 50.00, 60.00, 75.00, 100.00, 125.00, 150.00.

Garden Seats.

Frequently used in porches, greenhouses and gardens as seats and jardiniere stands. Not affected by dampness.

Chinese Glaze Garden Seats. In three assorted shapes: round, hexagon and square; in green, blue and buff; with open work sides in fancy cut out decorations; top 12 inches, height 20 inches, $3.75 each.

Sedji Garden Seat. Round, with corrugated or ribbed sides of green and blue, decorated in colored flowers; top 11 inches, height 20 inches, $6.75 each.

Chinese and Nankin Garden Seats. Blue and white floral decorations; regular barrel shape, top 11 inches, height 20 inches, $12.00 each.

Barrel Shape Garden Seats. With opening on each side for handles, decorated in dark rich coloring of flowers, birds and fancy ornamental treatments, or Persian patterns; height 22 inches, $18.00 each.

Round Barrel Shape Garden Seats. In rich colorings, Chinese decorations of flowers, birds and flowers, figure and landscape decorations, with fancy work on sides and top; $18.00 and $20.00.

Taizan Ware. Floral decoration of various colors. $45.00, 48.00, 75.00.

Bronze. Archaic decorations. $75.00 85.00, 150.00.

Cloisonne. 3 to 6 ft. high, in light and dark blues, black and red, with bird and flower decorations. $45.00, 55.00, 60.00, 75.00, 90.00, 100.00, 125.00, 150.00 and 200.00.

Satsuma Ware.

For many a year, the exquisite Satsumas of Japan have been reigning favorites with Occidental collectors, who never fail to be charmed with its gold, color, figure and floral decoration on crackle cream ground.

Boxes. In both low and high shapes, $9.50, 10.00, 20.00, 25.00.

Bowls. Small and large, $5.00, 10.00, 15.00, 16.50, 18.00, 20.00, 25.00, 30.00, 35.00, 40.00, 45.00, 50.00, 60.00.

Incense Burners. $12.00, 15.00, 18.00, 20.00, 25.00.

Jars. $12.00, 15.00, 18.00, 30.00.

Baskets. $13.50, 20.00, 30.00, 36.00.

Trays. $5.00, 8.00, 15.00, 20.00.

Vases $4.50, 5.00, 8.00, 10.00, 15.00, 22.00, 27.50, 35.00 to $180.50.

Placques. $25.00 to $75.00 each.

Koros. $7.50, 10.00, 15.00, 20.00 each.

Umbrella Jars. $45.00 and 55.00.

Solid Silverware.

From India, Japan and China.

Hand wrought in characteristic patterns—bamboo, foliage, figures, etc.

India Silver Tea sets,
India Silver Creamers,
India Silver Bowls,
India Silver Puff Boxes,
India Silver Salts,

India Silver Peppers,
India Silver Trays,
India Silver Bon-Bon Dishes,
India Silver Vases,
India Silver Jewel Boxes.

Japanese Silver Napkin Rings.

Chinese Silver Bowls,
Chinese Silver Goblets,

Chinese Silver Mugs,
Chinese Silver Coffee Spoons.

Oriental Jewelry.

An interesting collection of Oriental jewelry, mounted and unset, embracing:

Gold Rings, finely carved,
Scarf Pins, Hat Pins,
Turkish and India Necklaces,
Turkish Fobs,
Fobs with Crystal Balls,
Silver and Silver Gilt Turkish Bracelets,
India and Turkish Bangles (silver),
Chinese and Japanese Clasps,
Silver and Gold Lorgnette Chains,
Turkish Silver Clasps,
Turkish Silver Belts and Girdles,

Coral Strings,
Turkish Silver Collars
Turkish Silver Chain Purses,
Turkish Bag Clasps, Mounted with old Turkish embroidery
India Silver Cigarette Cases,
Enameled Clasps, Brooches
Old Turkish and Persian Embroidered Purses, Card Cases and Bags mounted with antique silver,
Lorgnette Chains in coral,
Lorgnette Chains with Baroque pearls.

Glossary

Arhat — *(See Rakan)*

Awaji School — Satsuma wares with a fine crackle generally embelished with transparent enamels.

Awataguchi — The Awata district of Kyoto.

Awata School — Satsuma wares finely crackled with a yellowy cream body tint generally decorated with polychrome enamels and gilt.

Bail handle — A handle looped from one side of an object to the other.

Bekko — Tortoiseshell glaze.

Benten — The only woman in the seven gods of good luck (Shichi fuku jin). She represents charity.

Biscuit — Clay which was fired but not glazed.

Bijin — A beautiful Japanese woman (or women).

Bishamon — One of the seven gods of good luck (Shichi fuku jin.). He holds a spear in one hand and a pagoda in the other. He represents glory.

Blank — A glazed but undecorated object.

Bodhisattva — *(See Bosatsu)*

Bosatsu — A Buddhist diety who by renouncing Buddhahood, works for the salvation of all beings.

Brocade — *(See Nishikide)*

Cha no yu — The tea ceremony.

Da wan — Teacup.

Cobalt oxide — Oxidized cobalt blue (used after 1870-72).

Conventional — Traditional style motif.

Daimyo — The lord of a fief having more than 10,000 koku. *(See koku)* The senior branch of the Tokugawa was the greatest daimyo.

Daikoku — One of the seven gods of good luck (Shichi fuku jin). He holds a hammer and is generally depicted standing on two rice sacks which sometimes resemble barrels. He represents wealth.

Diaper — A repetitive pattern.

Dragon — One of the four supernatural animals. The Japanese dragon is generally depicted with three claws and surrounded by lightning or flame symbols.

Dragon scale — *See Jakatsu*

Ebisu — One of the seven gods of good luck (Shichi fuku jin). He is depicted as a fisherman and is sometimes shown with either a basket of fish or a fish dangling from the end of a rod.

Enamel — Usually an opaque composition applied to the surface of pottery or porcelain, etc., and which is fused by firing.

En gobe — White or colored slip applied to earthenware either as a decoration or as a support for a glaze or enamel.

Firing — The process of applying heat.

Fudai — Daimyo who were vassals of the Tokugawa.

Fukurokuju — One of the seven gods of good luck (Shichi fuku jin). He has an elongated head and represents longevity.

Gosu (blue) — A blue which ranges in value and can be found in blue gray or blue black (akin to Prussian blue) and which was used prior to 1872.

Green ribboned medal — A government medal awarded to those who have contributed to Japanese society.

Hanne ike — A flower vase.

Hideyoshi (Toyotomi), 1526-1598 — In 1592 he became the military ruler of Japan.

Hotei — One of the seven gods of good luck (Shichi fuku jin). He is depicted as a rather fat man with a protruding stomach and represents contentment.

Ieyasu, 1542-1616 — The founder of the Tokugawa shogunate and member of the Tokugawa family.

Ito guri — A thread mark generally found running from left to right.

Jakatsu gusuri — A glaze run in large globules.

Jigger — A hollow mold used to form cups and bowls.

Jolley — A convex mold used to form dishes and plates.

Jurojin — One of the seven gods of good luck (Shichi fuku jin), similar to Fukurokuju.

Kame — The tortoise and one of the four supernatural animals.

Kannon — The deity of mercy.

Kara Shi Shi — A lion dog often depicted with a tama, symbolizing peace and longevity. When depicted in pairs the one with the open mouth is the female. Generally used as finials and handles.

Kiku mon — Chrysanthemoid form, it is an Imperial mon and has sixteen petals.

Kiln — An oven or heated enclosure used for firing.

Kiri mon — The mon of the Imperial family which incorporates the leaves of the *paulownia imperialis.*

Kirin — One of the four supernatural animals; it has a single horn and is the emblem of goodness.

Ko — Early.

Kogo — A small box (generally an incense holder or container).

Koku — A measure approximating 100-180 litre (used to measure the yield of rice of a particular land area).

Koro — An incense burner.

Kuro gusuri — A black glaze.

Kyoto School — Compromising the productions of Awata, Gojozaka, and Kyomizu.

Kyo yaki-Kyoto wares — A general name for the ceramics produced in Kyoto.

Lohan *(See Rakan)*

Luting — The joining of parts with slip.

Mahout — An elephant driver.

Maru mitsu aoi — The mon of the Tokugawa composed of three leaves of the asarum plant.

Mezzo relievo — A form of relief ornamentation in which the motif is cut from the wall of the object.

Mishima — Satsuma wares into which the motif has been incised or impressed and then filled with slip or enamel.

Mon — A family crest (heraldic bearing) badge.

Moriage — An embellishment formed by the addition of slip to the body of an object. Such is generally raised in relief.

Nihon/Nippon — Japan in the Japanese language.

Nishikide — Masses of color covering almost the entire surface of an object.

Nishikide diapers — Masses of polychrome diapers covering almost the entire surface of an object (on occasion may cover the entire surface).

No masks — Masks worn during the No dance drama.

Oni — A creature with an impish face, two horns, and usually dressed in a loin cloth. He is often shown escaping from Shoki.

Phoenix (Ho-o or Howo) — A favorite subject found on Satsuma, with its form adapted from Chinese art.

Rakan — The term used for lohan or arhat (Sanscrit). A rakan is a sage who has reached enlightenment and who is endowed with supernatural powers. Rakan are often depicted in groups and appear generally as emaciated, ragged, or austere figures.

Rokkasen — Generally five men and one woman. They are portrayed as a group of poets seated in a huddle.

Same gusuri — Shark's skin glaze.

Sanju rokkasen — The thirty-six poets. *(See Rokkasen)*

Satsuma — A faience, finely crackled and embellished with varying colored enamels.

Satsuma province — The fief of the Shimazu family located in the southern portion of the island of Kyushu. It is now Kagoshima prefecture.

Satsuma style — Porcelain wares with raised enamels and gilt embellishments.

Shimazu — The daimyo of Satsuma, Osumi, and part of Kiuga.

Shiro gusuri — White glaze.

Shogun — An Imperial office (seitai shogun). The Tokugawa were the greatest shoguns and were given full authority over the Japanese Empire by the Emperor.

Shoki — The demon killer (oni).

Slip — A mixture of clay and water used for decorating pottery. *(See Moriage).*

Sprigged on — Embellishing an object with molded-in-relief ornamentation by the luting method.

Sunkoroku — A gray pottery resembling stoneware.

Tama — The ball (pearl or jewel) associated with the Kara Shi Shi.

Tokyo — The capital of Japan formerly called Edo (Yedo).

Tora — The tiger.

Totai — Ceramic bodied cloisonne.

Yaki — Ware.

Yedo — *See Tokyo*

Bibliography

Books, English Text

Andacht, Sandra. *Satsuma an Illustrated Guide.* Des Moines: Wallace-Homestead Book Co., 1978.

Andacht, Garthe, Mascarelli. *Wallace-Homestead Price Guide to Oriental Antiques.* Des Moines: Wallace-Homestead Book Co., 1980.

Audsley, George, and Bowes, James. *Keramic Art of Japan.* London: H. Sotheran & Co., 1881.

Bolitho, Harold. *Meiji Japan.* London: Cambridge Univ. Press, 1977.

Brinkley, Capt. F. *Japan, Its History and Arts*, Vol. I-VIII. Tokyo: J.P. Millet, 1901.

Chisolm, L.W. *Fenollosa: The Far East and American Culture.* New Haven: Yale Univ. Press, 1963.

Cox, Warren. *Pottery and Porcelain.* New York: Crown Pub. Co., 1944.

Dillon, Edward. *Porcelain.* New York: G.P. Putnam's Sons, 1904.

Dillon, Edward. *The Arts of Japan.* London: Methuen & Co. Ltd., 1911.

Dilts, Marion. *The Pageant of Japanese History.* London: Longmans, Green and Co., 1938.

Fenollosa, Ernest F. *Epochs of Chinese and Japanese Art.* London: W. Heinemann, 1912.

Franks, Augustus W., Sir. *Japanese Pottery.* London: Chapman and Hall Ltd., 1885.

Fujioka, R. *Tea Ceremony Utensils.* Tokyo: Weatherhill, 1973.

Gorham, Hazel. *Japanese and Oriental Pottery.* Tokyo: Yamagato Printing Co.,

Hall, J.W. *Japan.* New York: Delacorte Press, 1970.

Hanover, Emil. *Potter and Porcelain.* (Trans. B. Rackham). London: 1925.

Hobson, R.L. *Handbook of the Pottery and Porcelain of the Far East in the British Museum.* London: 1924.

Honey, W.B. *The Ceramic Art of China and Other Countries in the Far East.* London: Faber, 1945.

Honey, W.B. *The Art of the Potter.* New York: Beechhurst Press, 1955.

Jenyns, Soame. *Japanese Pottery.* New York: F.A. Praeger, 1971.

Joly, Henri L. *Legend in Japanese Art.* Rutland: C. Tuttle Co., 1967.

Latourette, Kenneth. *History of Japan.* New York: Macmillan Co., 1967.

Miller, R.A. *Japanese Ceramics.* Rutland: C. Tuttle Co., 1960.

Okakura, Kakuzo. *The Book of Tea.* Tokyo: C. Tuttle Co., 1956.

Ragamey, Felix. *Japan, Its Art and Industry.* New York: Knickerbocker Press, 1893.

Reishauer, Edwin. *The Japanese.* Cambridge: Belknap Press, Harvard Univ., 1977.

Reishauer, Jean. *Early Japanese History,* Part B. Glouster: Princeton Univ. Press, 1967.

Roberts, John G. *Black Ships and Rising Sun.* New York: Simon and Schuster, 1971.

Roberts, L.P. *A Dictionary of Japanese Artists.* Tokyo: Weatherhill, 1976.

Sato, S. *Kyoto Ceramics.* Tokyo: Weatherhill, 1973.

Steward, Dick. *Arts and Crafts of Old Japan.* Chicago: A.C. McClurg & Co., 1906.

Walter, W.T. *Oriental Collections.* Baltimore: privately published, 1884.

Young, Jennie. *The Ceramic Art.* New York: Harper and Bros., 1878.

Japanese Texts

Egushi, Akira. *Tohei Nyumon.* Japan: Bunken Shuppan, 1979.

Koyama, R. *Nihon No Yakimono* (26 vols). Japan: Kodansha Intl., 1977-1979.

Onishi, Masataro. *Togei No Dento Giho.* Japan: Rukogakusha, 1978.

Catalogs

"ABC of Japanese Art." Board of Tourist Industry Japanese Government.
"Railways and Mr. Noritake Tsuda." Tokyo: Toppan Printing Co., 1937.
"Catalogue of the Morse Collection of Japanese Pottery." Boston: 1901.
"Chanoyu: Japanese Tea Ceremony." Japan Society, 1979.
"Chinese, Corean and Japanese Potteries." Japan Society, 1914.
"The One-Hundred Twenty Fourth Emperor of Japan," Enthronement Edition. Tokyo: *The Japan Advertiser Press,* Benjamin Flescher Editor & Publisher, Nov., 1928.
"Exhibition of Chinese, Japanese and Korean Art," Cambridge: Fogg Art Museum.
"Handbook of the Dept. of Oriental Art." Chicago: Art Institute of Chicago, 1933. Japan *Chronicle,* 1933-1934.
"Japan," Tokyo: Board of Tourist Industry, 1939.
"Japanese Pottery Old and New." Detroit: Detroit Institute of Arts, 1950.
"Oriental Art, Chinese and Japanese Objects." Morgan Collection, 1886.
"Pickard China and Glass." Chicago, 1917.
"The Charles Locke Collection." 1915.
"The Official Catalogue." Kyoto Commercial Museum, 1910.
"Vantine Catalogue." Circa 1885.
"Vantine Catalogue." Circa 1927.

Periodicals

Bing, S., and Sampson, Low. *Artistic Japan,* vols. 1-25. London: Marston, Searle and Rivington Ltd., May, 1888 through June, 1890.

Articles

Andacht, Sandra. "Satsuma." *Antique Trader Weekly,* June 29, 1977.
Andacht, Sandra. "Satsuma." *Antiques Monthly,* May, 1979.
Andacht, Sandra. "Satsuma." *Spinning Wheel* Magazine, May-June, 1980.
Andacht, Sandra. "Satsuma-Edo Period, Part I." *Orientalia Journal,* Nov., 1979.
Andacht, Sandra. "Kinkozan and Taizan." *Orientalia Journal,* Sept., 1980.
Andacht, Sandra. "Satsuma Export Wares, Meiji Period; an Argument for Acceptance." Oriental Art Society of Chicago *Newsletter,* supplement, May, 1978.
Andacht, Sandra. "Satsuma Blanks Decorated in the USA." *Orientalia Journal,* March, 1979.
Andacht, Sandra. "Satsuma — Japanese American." *Spinning Wheel* Magazine, May, 1979.
Garthe, Nancy Jean. "More on Cloisonné on Ceramics (Totai)." *Antique Trader Weekly,* Sept. 16, 1976.
Garthe, Nancy Jean. "Observations on Cloisonné — Cloisonné by Any Other Name: Totai, Part II." *Orientalia Journal,* July, 1980.
Shugio, H. "Japanese Art and Artists of Today." *Studio Magazine,* vol. 50, 1910.

Index

Photographs are identified in boldface type.

About the Author

Sandra Andacht resides with her husband Carl and their two sons Stuart and Jeffrey in a suburb of New York City. Sandra Andacht is the editor and publisher of *The Orientalia Journal.* Her column, ''East Meets West — Exploring Orientalia with Sandra Andacht'' is a regular feature of The *Antique Trader Weekly.* Mrs. Andacht has written *Satsuma: An Illustrated Guide* and co-authored the *Wallace-Homestead Price Guide to Oriental Antiques.* Numerous articles by her have been published in *The Orientalia Journal,* The *Antique Trader Weekly, Spinning Wheel* Magazine, *Antique Monthly,* and The Oriental Art Society of Chicago *Newsletter,* etc. She is a research consultant, lecturer, and appraiser and is called upon in this capacity by the United States Customs Service, among others.

KOREA

SEA of JAPAN

PACIFIC OCEAN

TSUSHIMA CHANNEL

Takatori ware

Karatsu ware

Nabeshima ware

IMARI

ARITA Imari ware

Kakiemon ware

KARATSU

Karatsu ware

FUKUOKA

FUKUOKA

SAGA

YAMAGUCHI

Hagi ware

SHIMANE

MATSUE

Sodeshi ware Rakuzan ware

Fujina ware

OKAYAMA

Bizen ware

KYOTO

Kyoto ware

Mushiage ware

Raku ware

OSAKA

Kosobe ware

INLAND SEA

Tobe ware

SHIKOKU I.

OTSURU

Onda ware

OITA

KYUSHU I.

NAESHIRO-GAWA

KAGOSHIMA

Satsuma ware

KAGOSHIMA

KAJIKI

Ryumonji ware